I *Still* BELIEVE

JEREMY CAMP

WITH DAVID THOMAS

W PUBLISHING GROUP

AN IMPRINT OF THOMAS NELSON

Published in Nashville, Tennessee, by W Publishing Group, an imprint of Thomas Nelson.

Thomas Nelson titles may be purchased in bulk for educational, business, fund-raising, or sales promotional use. For information, please e-mail SpecialMarkets@ThomasNelson.com.

Unless otherwise noted, Scripture quotations are taken from the Holy Bible, New International Version®, NIV®. © 1973, 1978, 1984, 2011 by Biblica, Inc.® Used by permission of Zondervan. All rights reserved worldwide.

Scripture quotations marked NASB are from New American Standard Bible®. © 1960, 1962, 1963, 1968, 1971, 1972, 1973, 1975, 1977, 1995 by The Lockman Foundation. Used by permission.

Scripture quotations marked NKJV are from the New King James Version®. © 1982 by Thomas Nelson. Used by permission. All rights reserved.

Scripture quotations marked KJV are from the King James Version. Public domain.

Any Internet addresses, phone numbers, or company or product information printed in this book is offered as a resource and is not intended in any way to be or to imply an endorsement by Thomas Nelson, nor does Thomas Nelson vouch for the existence, content, or services of these sites, phone numbers, companies, or products beyond the life of this book.

ISBN 978-0-7852-3342-8 (eBook)

Library of Congress Control Number: 2019952503

ISBN 978-0-7852-3341-1 (TP)

Printed in the United States of America

20 21 22 23 24 25   LSC   8 7 6 5 4 3 2 1

I STILL
BELIEVE

CONTENTS

Foreword by Bart Millard   VII

Prologue   IX

Chapter 1: It Starts at Home   I

Chapter 2: Tug-of-War   II

Chapter 3: Set Free   23

Chapter 4: The Call   31

Chapter 5: Heading West   43

Chapter 6: The Gift   53

Chapter 7: Broke-Up and Broken   65

Chapter 8: "Just One Person"   73

Chapter 9: Walking by Faith   81

Chapter 10: Seeking Hope   95

Chapter 11: "It's Time"   103

Chapter 12: Why?   115

Chapter 13: Breaking Through   129

Chapter 14: Falling in Love Again   141

Chapter 15: All About God   155

Chapter 16: Reaching the Roots   167

Chapter 17: All That Truly Matters   175

Chapter 18: There Will Be a Day   185

Chapter 19: Risking It All for the Gospel   197

Chapter 20: The Father's Perfect Love   211

Chapter 21: Lights! Camera! Action!   219

Chapter 22: I Still Believe   229

Notes   239

About the Author   241

FOREWORD

When I heard that Jeremy's book *I Still Believe* was going to be made into a movie, I was thrilled for him. I have known Jeremy since 2002, when we first toured together on Festival Con Dios. I was excited because I know how powerful a film can be in taking a story of God's grace to whole new audiences.

But if I'm being totally honest, I was also a bit nervous for him. When the movie *I Can Only Imagine* was released in 2017, depicting my life and all the hard things that went into the writing of the song, I didn't realize how difficult it was going to be for me and my family. It's humbling and frightening to see your life represented on the big screen. Actors are playing you, your family, and your friends. They're saying the things you said and doing the things you did— the good and the bad. You have the privilege of reliving some of the most incredible experiences of your life, but you also see your worst moments displayed on the screen for everyone to witness. Allowing the filmmakers to peel back the protective layers and show the history that went into the making of that song and the band MercyMe was one of the most vulnerable things I have ever done.

I know Jeremy shares the same fears and anxieties about seeing his life come to the big screen. I know how scared and excited he is. And I will be praying that God uses his powerful story to continue to build His kingdom.

It's hard to believe that a lifetime can be compressed into two hours or less of film. Hours and hours of footage (as well as a lifetime of moments) are left on the cutting room floor. I am thrilled that in the pages of this book, you have the chance to see the details of Jeremy's life that couldn't be included in the film.

Jeremy's story of loving and losing his wife Melissa—and the resilience and blessing that followed in his life with Adrienne—is a powerful testament to God's grace. As you'll read, Melissa's dying wish was that God would use her passing to bring just one person to faith. Jeremy's music and the beautiful way he's shared her story have brought many more than that into God's kingdom. And now, with the film about to release into theaters nationwide, I cannot wait to see what God is going to do with it.

—BART MILLARD, 2019

PROLOGUE

Pick up your guitar.

I didn't want to. I didn't want anything to do with music. It had been two weeks since Melissa had gone to heaven. My wife was only twenty-one, and we had been married just three and a half months when she passed away from ovarian cancer.

I sat on the couch in my parents' living room alone—alone in many ways.

For two weeks my life had been a fog that wouldn't lift. After everything had seemed to make so much sense, now nothing made sense. Doctors had told us Melissa's cancer was gone. We had married with the dream of having kids and working together in ministry—me through music, her through women's ministries and Bible studies. But then we barely had the chance to begin living out our dream.

My Melissa was gone, and I wondered where God was. I wanted to pray, but in my despair I wasn't even sure what my own thoughts were. I tried to pray, but I didn't know where to begin. Whatever weak words I did manage to send God's way seemed to be getting lost in the fog engulfing me.

Do You really hear me, God?

Do You really care about every situation?

God? Are You near?

Pick up your guitar: For the first time since Melissa's death, I felt like God was answering me. His words came crystal clear into my heart.

But I didn't want to pick up my guitar. I didn't want to go back to music, or to anything I had done before. When I would write songs, I would write what my heart felt. Except now I felt nothing. I was numb. I was physically and emotionally drained. I had nothing to offer.

No, Lord—no. The last thing I want to do is play my guitar.

Pick up your guitar. I have something for you to write.

I relented and began mindlessly strumming some chords. I didn't understand why I was playing, but I kept going. Then emotions began to well up within me. I felt tears forming in my eyes. Words—actual thoughts—came to me, and I began to speak them as I played.

Scattered words and empty thoughts
Seem to pour from my heart

For the first time in two weeks, I was able to express how I felt.

I've never felt so torn before
Seems I don't know where to start

I quickly found a pen and notebook and returned to the couch.

But it's now that I feel Your grace fall like rain
From every fingertip, washing away my pain

I jotted down the words as they continued to come to me.

I still believe in Your faithfulness
I still believe in Your truth
I still believe in Your holy Word

The words were pouring out, not from my mind but from deep within my soul.

Even when I don't see, I still believe

I alternated between playing the tune and writing in the notebook until I softly sang and penned the final words:

In brokenness I can see that this was Your will
for me. Help me to know You are near.[1]

I leaned back, struck by the words that had come to me, and completely unaware of how God would use those words to speak through me to others who, like me, felt abandoned in life's deepest valley. Who needed hope. Who needed encouragement to allow God to dig into the depths of their souls, down to the very foundation of their faith, and then discover the resolve to declare, "I still believe!"

I wrote "I Still Believe" in ten minutes.

But, in essence, I had been writing the song for all my life.

Chapter 1

IT STARTS AT HOME

*F*aith and family.

When I look back, it's fitting that my healing in the aftermath of Melissa's passing began to take place back in my parents' home in Lafayette, Indiana.

I had left home for California to attend Bible college. It was in California that I found my path in ministry. It was there that my music career began to develop. It was there that I met God's partner for me in ministry. But after Melissa's memorial service, when the path I thought had been laid out in front of me suddenly disappeared, when my faith had been shaken in a manner I had never imagined possible, all I knew to do was to go home.

Faith and family are seamlessly knit together in my life's story.

My parents provided me with what they did not have growing up: a Christian home. That in itself was a miracle.

Imagine a drunken man, with his equally loaded friend, staggering into a church on a Sunday evening and then answering an altar call to accept Jesus as his Savior, and you have my dad's remarkable conversion story.

My dad, Tom—or "Bear," as his friends called him—dropped

out of school at age sixteen because he had gotten heavily into alcohol and drugs. (He later earned his GED and attended college.) My dad has a life-of-the-party, let's-have-some-fun-here personality, and when he was growing up, he didn't have any trouble finding the parties or convincing others to join in his type of fun.

My mom, Teri, was the classic good girl in school. She grew up in a stable home environment. A good student, she had plans and goals. She had been accepted to Purdue University when she met and began dating my dad her senior year of high school.

Their relationship was the talk of the hallways—but not in the head-cheerleader-dates-the-quarterback kind of way. The comments were more like "What is *she* doing going out with *him*?"

She had fallen for my dad's likable personality and found him easy to talk to. But because of his heavy drinking and marijuana use, my dad had trouble landing steady work. So my mom scrapped her plans to study interior decorating in college and started working instead. My parents became popular party hosts. My dad was into selling pot by then, so you can imagine the types of parties and partygoers at my parents' home.

After learning my mom was pregnant, they moved in together, and my sister, April, was born out of wedlock in 1975. Having a newborn cut back on the parties in the home, but my dad's lifestyle continued further down the wrong path. His drinking increased, and he began to use and sell cocaine. The more he drank, the more violent he became.

About a year and a half after April was born, my dad was battling depression and realized his life was spiraling out of control.

"I don't know what's wrong with me," he told my mom. "I feel so empty inside. It's not you. It's not April. The drugs aren't making me happy. I don't know what's wrong."

"Do you need to see a psychiatrist?" my mom asked him.

"No," my dad replied. "I need to talk to a minister."

On Christmas Day 1976, my dad was noticeably depressed. My

mom thought he might harm himself, but when she tried to console him, my dad said, "I have to go to church and I have to go now."

They drove from church to church that evening, looking for one that was open. Finally, they found one where a couple of people were inside practicing music. My parents walked in and quietly sat in a pew, but the musicians never spoke to them, probably because they looked more like hippies than regular churchgoers. My parents remained in the pew for a while until my mom asked my dad if he felt better.

"Yes," he said, and they left.

Four days later, on a Wednesday evening, my parents again decided to look for a church.

When my dad was young, a sweet neighbor lady named Meb had taken him to church with her from time to time. One of those times, when my dad was eleven, he had gone forward to accept Christ. Without a family to keep him spiritually connected, though, he eventually got away from church. He had brought up spiritual topics with my mom early in their relationship, but Christianity stayed something he thought about and questioned in his heart and never became more than that. But at least he had that church background Meb had provided him when he analyzed his own life and reached the conclusion that he needed to make a serious change. He had tried just about everything else, but deep in his heart he knew what the truth was and that the Holy Spirit was drawing him and doing a deep work within him.

My mom had attended churches in spurts when she was growing up, with her mom taking her and her dad staying home, except on Easter Sundays and a few other special occasions. Her mother had bought a book of Bible stories that my mom had enjoyed reading as a child. But while she knew about Jesus, there was never a time when my mom had a relationship with Him. With my dad showing just enough of a trend toward dangerous behavior, she was open to church providing the source for the change he needed.

It was a few days after Christmas, and my dad said again, "I have to talk to a minister. I know where we can go—Meb will be at church."

My dad knew where his former neighbor would be on a Wednesday night. When they arrived at the church, the service had just ended and people were on their way out. As expected, Meb was there. A big smile crossed her face when she saw my dad. When my dad said he needed to talk to a minister, she introduced my parents to her pastor. The four of them sat down, and my dad explained his problems and described how he felt a void in his life. The pastor identified the problem as unconfessed sin and explained that the void my dad felt was one that only Christ could fill. My dad agreed. The pastor then led my parents through a prayer asking for forgiveness, although my mom prayed more out of embarrassment and the potential awkwardness of not praying in that small of a group.

After the prayer, the pastor gave my parents a short and direct list of changes they needed to make: "You need to get married, change the way you dress, cut your hair, and get new friends."

My parents understood the need to give up the drugs and alcohol. But they were confused about how they could just come up with a completely new set of friends overnight. And as for the way they dressed, they could barely afford the clothes they did have. How were they supposed to afford an all-new wardrobe?

My dad initially had a problem with marriage. He had been briefly married when he was sixteen. His girlfriend got pregnant, so they married. But when she had a miscarriage, they decided they didn't want to be together and divorced after less than six months together. There had been a few times in the past when my dad had asked my mom if she would marry him if he asked. She kept saying she would, but my dad never asked. He told my mom he had no interest in marrying because he had never seen a good marriage—not growing up and not for the few months he was married. But as he considered what the pastor had said about needing to marry, he agreed.

The pastor gave my parents a Bible, but he didn't give them any practical help for how to make the changes he told them they must make.

As a result, they left the church asking themselves, *How can we do all that?*

Changed for Good

The Bible the pastor had given my parents was a King James Version. Reading was difficult for my dad, and the King James was even more of a challenge, so my mom read from the Bible to him. They continued to talk about church, and my mom mentioned that coworkers had been talking to her about Jesus and had said my parents would be welcomed at their church regardless of how they looked or dressed. My dad agreed to try it.

They planned to attend the Assemblies of God church on the first Sunday evening of the new year—January 2, 1977. My dad had helped a friend move that morning, then went out with his friend that afternoon.

As my mom was getting ready for church, he called. "Where are you?" she asked him.

"I'm at a Mexican restaurant."

She knew he was at the only local restaurant that served beer on Sundays. "Have you been drinking?"

"Oh, just a little."

When my dad came home to pick her up for church, he and his friend were laughing about how they had been busting out lights at the restaurant. They had been drinking more than "just a little." My mom started crying. From the night they had prayed at Meb's church, neither of them had used drugs or alcohol—not even on New Year's Eve. "There's no way I'm going to church with you guys," she told him.

My mom's mother was keeping April that evening, so when my mom saw how drunk my dad and his friend were, she immediately left for church alone.

Because it was a Sunday evening, the crowd of about three hundred wasn't as large as for a Sunday morning service. About eight rows of folding chairs at the back of the sanctuary had been roped off so the people would sit closer to the front. My mom took a seat by herself in the middle of the last available row. Shortly after the service began, she heard a commotion behind her. She looked over her shoulder to see my dad and his friend stumbling through the doors in the back.

My mom's first reaction was to try to hide. She turned back toward the front, slumped in her seat, and tried to blend in with the others in front of her. It didn't work. My dad and his friend spotted my mom and started making their way toward her. But not by walking down the aisle and quietly slipping through the row where my mom was sitting. My dad started off on the most direct route from point A to point B—by stepping over the roped-off rows of chairs!

My mom continued to look forward while everyone else turned their attention to the two drunken chair-jumpers. My dad and his friend plopped down right next to my embarrassed mom, and the friend started chattering away.

An usher seeking to calm the ruckus came over and asked my dad's friend if he would like to go sit next to him, and my dad's drinking buddy obliged.

Up front, the pastor talked about being delivered from the bondage of drugs and alcohol. A couple of times during the message, my dad's friend left his seat, ran over to my dad, said, "Man, Bear, this guy knows what he's talking about!" and then ran back to his seat next to the usher.

As the pastor preached, my mom noticed tears rolling from my dad's eyes. The pastor's words really struck home with my dad, who cried throughout the message.

When the pastor concluded and asked if anyone would like to come to the altar to ask Jesus into their heart, my dad's friend ran forward while my parents hesitated, both thinking, *Haven't we done this already?* When a youth pastor approached and offered to take them to the front if they wanted to answer the pastor's call, they stood and made their way down the aisle too. The congregation gathered around the three of them at the altar and prayed for them. With all of them crying, my mom at that point was just relieved that the guys were going to change. My dad was immediately delivered from drugs and alcohol and walked out of that church sober.

My parents later learned that alcoholics and hippies were the pastor's least-favorite types of people, but he still had welcomed my dad and his friend into the church that night. The church members had been praying for a revival to break out in their church, and one began that night when, of all people, two drunk hippies answered the altar call. God does work in mysterious ways!

The pastor wound up having many opportunities to share what he would call the "whosoever ministry," exhorting the body of Christ to minister to whomever God brought into their path.

Instead of focusing on outward things, the members of that church encouraged my parents to get into the Word and into fellowship with other believers. They gave my parents a copy of The Living Bible to take home and suggested they begin reading in the gospel of John. John's manner of expressing the love that Jesus had demonstrated for all mankind through His death and resurrection deeply impacted my mom's heart. She had a revelation that, like my dad had been, she also was a sinner in need of salvation. One night, in her favorite living room chair, she said, "Lord, I am sorry." That became her life-changing moment. She asked Jesus to come into her heart and prayed, "I will go anywhere, do anything. Whatever You ask, I'm Yours."

Quite fitting, considering their contrasting personalities. My dad came to Christ in a public, very emotional setting. My mom did so in a private, quiet moment. Yet the immediate impact of their decisions was the same: their lives were completely changed. On January 22, 1977, in that same Assemblies of God church, they were married. From that day forward, they modeled the type of relationship that God prescribed in Scripture and poured the foundation of faith on which I would be raised.

I was born almost a year later, on January 12, 1978. Eight years later, April and I were joined by our brother Jared. Two years after that, Joshua came along. Josh was born with Down syndrome, and he was a blessing who completed our family in more ways than one.

Our parents' decisions to become Christians certainly didn't lead to a life of smooth sailing for them and our family. It was just the opposite, in fact, because we encountered our share of struggles. And not all of us kids always walked the path our parents wanted us to follow.

But all along our journey together, we always knew where to turn for answers to life's questions: to God's Word and to one another. And that pattern has remained unchanged as we Camp kids have progressed into adulthood and started our own families. Our family has incredible stories of God's loving mercy.

Learning at Home

Before my dad dropped out of high school, he had a difficult time focusing on reading—probably from his abuse of drugs and alcohol. I remember as I grew up, however, that my dad was constantly reading the Bible. He said because of his struggles in school, he had hated to read books before becoming a Christian. But he certainly loved to spend time studying God's Word. In fact, for a short time we lived in Springfield, Missouri, so my dad could attend Central Bible College and prepare for entering full-time ministry.

I remember our family always being heavily involved in church. We were one of those families that was in church practically every time the doors were unlocked. My parents attended and led Bible studies. We would have friends over to our house, and my dad would play his guitar and lead worship right there in our living room. My mom and dad shared their faith with anyone they met, telling them about the complete transformation God had made in their lives.

The impression of my parents that remains with me is how real they were. They were the same at home as they were in church. They wouldn't go to church and worship with raised hands, talk like a Christian should, and then return home and act or speak differently. They didn't compartmentalize. They were who they were because that was who they were; the changes God made in their hearts were complete and reflected in every area of their lives. I credit my parents' consistency in living the Christian lifestyle as the reason I never became jaded toward Christianity growing up, not even during the years when I wandered from the straight and narrow path.

The phrase "He has a shepherd's heart" perfectly describes my dad. He is a great listener who truly cares about people. I remember people sitting in our living room and pouring out their hearts, and he would sit there and not just listen but intently listen. He is such a people person, and people obviously love being around him.

My dad is hilarious too. After becoming a Christian, he remained the life of the party—just different types of parties. We would go camping—yes, the Camps went camping—and my dad would make up hilarious songs around the campfire. To get the whole family involved, he'd pester us to echo the silly lyrics he improvised. One time we all went roller-skating, and he went dressed in overalls with shorts over them just to be goofy and see if he could embarrass us.

My mom was more prim and proper. She wasn't outwardly emotional (except when she saw the Lord at work), and she was meticulous. I used to think it took her forever to put her makeup on. It seemed like she wrote slowly, too, but when she finished, her handwriting was flawless.

She kept the house clean and organized because, like my dad, she enjoyed having friends over and hosting Bible studies and prayer groups. And my mom was dedicated to praying. I remember many, many times walking into a room and seeing her facedown on the floor, praying and interceding.

My parents were opposites attracted to each other, but through Christ their opposite ways complemented one another. My dad had a go-for-it attitude. If he felt God wanted him to do something, he was ready to go. My mom would say, "We need to make sure about this, so let's pray about it a little more." My personality is closer to my dad's, but from my mom I learned the importance of discipline and steadiness in the Christian lifestyle.

When we kids encountered problems, our parents would encourage us with words and wisdom from Scripture—not just with their own words and advice. Prayer time was prioritized because our home was a home of prayer. We often prayed together as a family. When we had needs, whether as an individual or as a group, we prayed about them. And we definitely had needs.

Chapter 2

TUG-OF-WAR

Our family was not just poor but super poor. Before he became a Christian, my dad's alcohol and drug use had prevented him from holding down steady jobs. After my parents became saved, their priorities changed to God and laying a foundation for our family. Because my dad did not have a strong educational background, the better jobs available to him were factory positions that often would have required long hours and working on Sundays. He chose instead to take construction-type jobs that enabled him to spend more time with our family and remain in fellowship with other believers. Those jobs also often meant being laid off, especially during the winter.

It is no exaggeration to say there were days when our cupboards were bare, and we knew they would stay that way until my dad's next paycheck. As a family, we would pray for food, and I remember nights when we prayed and the next morning there would be a bag of groceries on our front step. As far as I knew, my parents weren't telling anyone that we were out of food. But God knew, and He would place our grocery needs on someone's heart. Many times, we had no idea who had brought us food, but we always knew that it was provided by God.

Our electricity and water were cut off a few times because we couldn't pay the bills. When the electricity was off, we would make do with candlelight and oil lights until the next paycheck came.

In one house we lived in, a wood-burning stove in our basement provided heat. The basement was creepy to me—it felt like an underground cavern—and even when my dad was out working and I was the oldest male in the house, I was too afraid to go down into the basement to light the stove. My mom didn't like going down there, either. I would study or read in my upstairs bedroom while wrapped in blankets because I was so cold. But there was no way I was going down to that basement.

Once when we were without electricity and couldn't flush the toilet because our water ran on a pump, we had to get a bucket of snow and dump it into the toilet tank so we could flush. I remember when we ran out of toilet paper and either didn't have the money to buy more or had to save what little money we did have for greater needs. Our parents taught us to make toilet paper out of newspapers by crunching up the pages and rubbing them together to soften them for use.

Sometimes we had to scrape together money for my dad to buy gas so he could drive to work. April and I would contribute any change we happened to have accumulated. We would pool together our change, count it on the table, and tell our dad, "Okay, here's $3.50."

We didn't have to live that way all the time, but it happened enough that I have clear memories of what those experiences were like.

We wore a lot of hand-me-downs, but our parents did their best to make sure we had what we needed. If one of us needed a pair of jeans or shoes, we'd go get them. Every once in a while we would have enough money to eat out at a place such as Wendy's, and eating out—even if it was fast food—was a real treat.

Paycheck to paycheck, my parents lived by faith. I would closely watch them and be amazed at their faith during difficult circumstances that I knew had to be stressful. I remember times when our needs were great, and my dad would pull out his guitar and lead us in a time of family worship. Despite the circumstances, he would play and sing with such incredible joy. For my parents, God truly was good all the time.

I needed my parents' example. As I started working my way through elementary school, I began to realize how our situation compared to those of families of others my age. As that realization set in, I became embarrassed because we were poor.

Our school took part in the governmental program that provided free lunches for kids from low-income families. To have my name on the free-lunch list was especially embarrassing. In seventh grade, I believe it was, I was so ashamed that I would beg my parents to give me money so I could be seen buying lunch instead of having my food given to me.

I once wore the same shirt twice in a week, and when another student pointed that out, I was so humiliated that I wanted to hide. But I never resented our situation. I knew my parents worked hard to make as much money as they could for us, and they left no doubt that their faith was in God to provide. And each time He met our needs, by whatever means it was, they made sure we kids knew it was God who had provided.

Even the Pintos.

Giving and Receiving

Cars were among the gifts that people blessed us with, and we sure had some interesting vehicles. People were gracious in offering us cars, but, of course, they weren't the types of cars that we would be able to use for years and years. We would drive one for as long as we could, then God would put it in someone else's heart to give us our next vehicle. We were thankful to have each one we received. One of our cars was a beat-up, sad little orange Ford Pinto.

My mom drove it one day to pick up April and a couple of her friends from a Girl Scouts meeting. As my mom drove home, she could see in the rearview mirror that one of April's friends was big eyed as she surveyed the interesting characteristics of the car's interior.

"Um, where did you get this car?" April's friend asked.

"Oh, a friend gave it to us," my mom answered.

The girl resumed her inspection before saying just loud enough for my mom to hear, "Hmm, some friend."

My mom chuckled and kept motoring down the road in the free Pinto.

I remember another car—also an orange Pinto—that my mom was driving when she picked me up at church. I hopped in and looked down to see the ground under my feet. The passenger-side floorboard was so rusted that there were big holes in the floor.

I closed the door and noticed a belt hanging from it. "What's this?" I asked.

"Buckle up and hold on to the belt," my mom told me, "because if you don't, the door will fly open when we go around curves."

That was one instance when obeying my mom was easy. I held a firm grip on that belt all the way home.

When I reached junior high, playing sports helped make me pretty popular among my classmates. I actually was too cool for my own good, but that will be addressed later.

One day after school, I was talking with my girlfriend while waiting on my dad to pick me up. *Girlfriend* is actually too strong of a word to describe our relationship. We were "going out," if you remember that phrase, even though we weren't going out anywhere. But at the time it seemed like a serious relationship. Not only was she my girlfriend, but she was also a cheerleader. So there I was, the popular football player, trying to look all cool while talking to my cheerleader girlfriend, when I heard a loud car entering the parking lot.

I turned, as did all the others around me, and saw my dad pulling up in yet another Pinto—a red one this time—someone had given us. The car had lost its muffler sometime before, so there was no discreetly pulling up to the school.

The Pinto was rusted and beat up, and I felt like everyone outside the school was watching as I walked over to it. I grabbed the passenger-side door handle and pulled. It wouldn't budge. I gave it another yank while trying to look like it wasn't my second attempt. Still nothing. I had to crawl through the window and into the seat. Trust me, there's no way to do that without being noticed. Especially because I was a popular athlete in school, I dealt with embarrassment a great deal, but I didn't resent our family's financial situation. I wished that we could have better cars and that we wouldn't have to go to secondhand stores to purchase clothes, but because of my parents' attitude, I had no resentment.

All along they worked hard and taught us about having faith in God, to believe He would meet our needs. And He did, countless times over.

We weren't able to have many of the things we wanted, but that taught us to appreciate the times when we did receive things on our lists of wants.

Christmas was a big deal in our home. I always had trouble sleeping Christmas Eve night and invariably would wake up around three in the morning and ask my parents, "Can we please get up? Can we please get up?" They would send me back to bed, though, and I would have to wait until a more decent hour to get up and see what gifts we had.

My parents would be excited about Christmas, too, because they had saved up whatever money they could for gifts to make Christmas morning special for all of us.

One gift I distinctly recall receiving demonstrates how we learned to appreciate what others our age might consider a small gift. I was big into sports growing up, and one Christmas I received a Nike duffel bag for all my sports gear. I was so excited. I carried that bag anytime I had a reason to haul my equipment around.

While the bag was nice to receive and very practical, what meant more was the knowledge that my parents had worked odd jobs and saved up their money to give me a gift I didn't have to have.

I hope that my children still have the same appreciation that I did when I was young. Even though I'm in a different financial position from what my parents were in, my wife and I want our children to have a full appreciation of how the gifts they receive on Christmas morning are blessings from God. That lesson is probably easier to teach when a family has fewer resources as my family did growing up.

Although my parents did not have a lot of material resources, they still were giving people. They were great at giving others time and attention—two resources people often fail to realize they have to offer.

In addition to the Bible studies and church groups they took part in, my parents also served as caretakers for troubled boys.

When I was six, they started working with a group home to provide a home for teenage boys who had been in trouble. As many as eight boys stayed with us at one time, and some of the kids came from really tough backgrounds.

Originally my parents were told it would be okay if they shared Christ with the boys, but only if the boys asked about Him. When my parents shared the gospel with the boys who did show interest, however, the group home disapproved.

Because of that, my parents left the program after almost a year. My dad took a job as a childcare worker at a home for boys, so my parents were constantly bringing in boys and even some adults who needed help. I remember an elderly woman in a wheelchair who lived with us for a while. I also remember a truant officer who would call my parents often to ask if we could take in another troubled boy. And our pastor would contact my parents about people he knew who needed a place to stay.

On a couple of different occasions, I even contributed kids to the Camps' program. They weren't even close friends of mine, but I knew they had difficult home situations, and I asked my parents if they could stay with us.

"If you don't mind sharing a room with them," they told me.

I was fine with that, and when their parents agreed to let them live with us for a while, I had new roommates.

My parents had a heart for troubled people—especially youth—and wanted to provide a stable home environment that most of them didn't have. They did that even though we were struggling financially.

God always met our needs, though.

There was one teenager named Todd who lived with us. Todd was a big kid who could really eat. One day he opened the refrigerator, and there wasn't much on the shelves.

"Teri," he asked my mom, "what are we going to have for supper?"

"Don't worry about it," my mom told him. "There's food in there you just can't see."

Todd gave her a strange look and shut the refrigerator door.

As dinnertime neared, my mom put together everything she could find in the refrigerator and in the cabinets. When Todd came to the kitchen table, he did a double take when he saw a full spread of a wide variety of foods. Todd ate all he could and left the table amazed that so much food had come out of what had looked like so little.

No matter how accustomed our family became to seeing God provide, each instance still surprised us a bit. We truly understood that God always was meeting our needs.

The Battle Within

My mom likes to tell the story of one time when someone gave us a freezer full of liver. We ate a lot of liver for a while, and my mom remembers praying, "Oh, Lord, I just wish we had something different to eat."

Shortly after praying that, she read in Deuteronomy where the Israelites were reminded of how the Lord had provided for them in the desert. The Israelites had grumbled and complained because the Lord had kept giving them manna to eat and they had grown tired of eating the same thing over and over.

As my mom was reading, the Lord reminded her, *I'm providing for you. I am doing this to test you and to know what's in your heart and to humble you. Then, when you come into the land of plenty, you won't forget Me.*

It hit my mom that God was providing for our needs and that our needs weren't what the typical American would consider needs. My mom had not been raised in an environment of want. Her family had plenty in their household. They took nice vacations and stayed in nice hotels. It was nothing like the way we were growing up.

But almost from the day my mom had become a Christian, she looked at times of need with this question in mind: What would it be like to be a missionary? She thought of missionaries and the conditions in which some of them chose to live in order to take the gospel message to the unsaved, and she chose to look at her surroundings with a "Think missionary" mind-set. To this day, when she hears someone describing a seemingly difficult set of circumstances, she will make the quote marks sign with her fingers raised, and say, "Think missionary."

With all the different people moving into and out of our homes, my parents were very careful to make sure that we, as their kids, received the proper parent-children attention we needed. I don't recall ever thinking the other kids were taking away from something I should have had in our home. Looking back now, I understand that living with kids from difficult backgrounds perhaps helped me keep proper perspective on what I did have at home in my parents' time and attention, instead of what I did not have in material goods.

Still, though, I made some poor decisions in response to the circumstances we faced growing up.

At age four or five, I had asked Jesus into my heart, and I had grown up a good churchgoing boy. Beginning in junior high and into my high school years, though, I began to stray for the first time.

I excelled in sports, and I worked out a lot and was in good shape. When I reached the age when I could play team sports in school—especially football—my athletic ability afforded me a "cool" status on campus.

I set out on a course to prove that I could do whatever I wanted to do. I honestly don't think I was going through some sort of ultra-rebellious stage, because I don't know what I would have been rebelling against. I wasn't angry at my parents. I wasn't angry at the church. Even though we were poor, I wasn't angry at what some would call "the system." But I think that after growing up in humble surroundings, being a popular athlete in school made me want to test how far I could stretch my boundaries. I had missed out on some pleasures at home that my friends had enjoyed, I thought, so now I was going to have some fun. If anything, I actually was insecure and trying to be accepted.

I wound up in an internal tug-of-war. I knew what was right and was influenced positively at home with my parents and at church. Yet at the same time, my desire to be part of the "in" crowd was pulling me in the opposite direction.

To appease the "be cool" side of me, I started partying and drinking alcohol. When I drank, I'd feel much braver, and I almost got into several fights. Because I was one of the strongest boys in my class, there really weren't any takers for fights, so mostly I would put on a display of macho bravado knowing I probably wouldn't have to back it up. Although I wouldn't have minded if someone did dare to challenge me.

I also used my status and strength to stand up for those who were picked on. I wasn't really interested in trying to gain acceptance from the super-popular kids—I wasn't among the coolest of the cool and didn't care to be. Still, I did run with the popular crowd; but because I had been an underdog for much of my life to that point, I kept an eye out for opportunities to protect the poorer or less-popular kids who were ridiculed. If I saw someone in the underdog group being picked on, I'd step in and tell the bully to stop, and usually he would without me having to become the enforcer. Although I wasn't always doing good things, I still had a lot of do-good in me.

I didn't turn my back on God. I still went to church and did the "church thing." One trait I admired about my parents was their intentionality in behaving the same away from church as they did at church.

I didn't lose my sense of right and wrong. I knew the truth. If I was going out to a party, I liked to drink a little before I got there so I'd already be a little numbed to the feeling of conviction I'd get while I was at the party.

At church I would feel convicted about the wrong decisions I was making. I would tell God that I was sorry and that I wanted to change. But then I would go to school the next morning and want to do the same old things that the others were doing. I wanted to do right, but at the same time I could not say no to what I knew was wrong.

It was the type of internal battle that Paul wrote about in Romans 7:21–25:

Although I want to do good, evil is right there with me. For in my inner being I delight in God's law; but I see another law at work in me, waging war against the law of my mind and making me a prisoner of the law of sin at work within me. What a wretched man I am! Who will rescue me from this body that is subject to death? Thanks be to God, who delivers me through Jesus Christ our Lord!

I discovered that in my pursuit of having fun, I was only having some fun. The fun times weren't lasting. They couldn't last because, as I knew in my heart, the source of my fun was outside of God's will. And I would come to learn that the peace that comes from having fun inside of God's will is far better.

Chapter 3

SET FREE

My dad had a guitar that he would play in our house during our family worship and devotional times, and he often led worship at church. Even though his guitar was usually in plain sight at home, I had never felt curious about trying to play it because sports—especially football—were my main interest.

One day when I was fourteen, though, I asked my dad if he could show me how to play a few chords. When he helped place the fingers of my left hand in the proper spots on the guitar's fretboard and I stroked my right thumb down across the strings, the sweet sound of that one chord sounded like a complete masterpiece.

"This is awesome!" I told my dad.

It's difficult to explain, but having my hands on a guitar just felt natural. With my dad teaching me what he had learned on his own, I quickly began picking up the basics of playing. The guitar didn't replace sports, but I did enjoy trying to learn how to play songs.

With a knack for playing by ear—the ability to hear songs and figure out the chords without the aid of written music—I started playing songs I had heard. Songs with a rock edge to them were my favorites.

Secular music wasn't allowed in our home, but when my parents were out of the house, I would turn on the radio and crank up a classic rock or Top 40 radio station. I got in trouble once for changing into a Lenny Kravitz T-shirt after I left our house. I changed back out of the shirt before I got home, but my mom somehow found out and got mad at me.

"How can you wear something like that?" she wanted to know. I began playing songs I heard on the radio by mainstream artists such as Pearl Jam, Aerosmith, and Creedence Clearwater Revival. From the Christian music I listened to at home (when my mom or dad were there), I also picked up songs by Mylon LeFevre & Broken Heart, DeGarmo & Key, and Resurrection Band.

Music was a big part of our family time. In addition to worshipping together and playing Christian CDs at home, our family attended the big Christian music festivals Ichthus (in Kentucky) and Cornerstone (in Illinois). I remember attending one Cornerstone festival and thinking, *Someday, it would be cool to sing on that stage.* Of course, I also would watch a college or pro-football game on TV and think, *Someday, it would be cool to play on that field.*

As picking up the musical elements of songs became more natural, I began noticing how the lyrics of some songs seemed to tell the story of the writer's life. I could tell that music could be an outlet for an artist's feelings and emotions and began to take note of how my emotions began to stir as I played.

During one of those tugs-of-war between knowing right and doing wrong, for the first time I wrote the words to my own song.

The song started with me looking in a mirror, seeing a figure whose life was all bent out of shape and in total despair, and then telling the Lord, "You got to set me free from sin." It included lines that stated where I was at that moment in my life: "Whenever I come close to You, I turn back to sin." I titled the song "Set Me Free." And my first performance of it was for my parents, right after I wrote it. They listened and afterward read over the words very carefully.

Up to that point I had hidden my partying and drinking from my parents. One time, when I had been out drinking with a friend, my friend had drunk a lot more than I had and was in no condition to drive. Even though I wasn't exactly sober and was too young to have a driver's license, I drove ten or fifteen minutes to my house. When we walked in the door, I told my parents, "We're tired. We're going to crash upstairs."

Driving home that night was one of those decisions I'd love to do over. I should have just called my parents to come get us. The consequences would have been far less than if I had been caught driving under the influence and without a license. My parents later told me they knew I was wandering into potentially dangerous areas during that time, but they had no idea how far I had gone because I had been careful to make sure they didn't find out.

I wasn't rebelling against them—I was just doing my own thing. If I had been rebelling, I would have wanted them to know at least some of what I was doing. But that wasn't the case because I didn't want to hurt them. I didn't want to disappoint my parents or let them down.

As my mom and dad read the lyrics of "Set Me Free," serious looks came over their faces.

"That is pretty heavy," my dad said. "Are you okay?"

They've caught me! I immediately thought. I went into cover mode.

"I was thinking of April when I wrote that," I said.

My sister was doing her own thing too. Except she had gone further than me, even getting into drugs for a while. Plus, my parents knew more about what she was doing than what I was doing. "Okay," my parents said, and I hid a sigh of relief at dodging getting busted that time.

But I couldn't dodge the message in my first song.

Pushing the Reset Button

The summer after my sophomore year at McCutcheon High School in Lafayette, I attended a weeklong summer camp in California.

My dad had started Harvest Chapel in Lafayette when I was fourteen. Harvest is a Calvary Chapel church and part of the fellowship of nondenominational churches that began in 1965 with the Calvary Chapel in Costa Mesa, California, pastored by Chuck Smith. Because the church was new and small, there wasn't a youth group yet, so I attended the youth group at the Calvary Chapel we had attended in Crawfordsville, about thirty miles from Lafayette. The association of Calvary Chapels had a summertime youth camp in California that attracted teenagers from across the country, and my youth group went to the camp. We held fund-raisers to raise money for the trip, and someone sponsored me to cover my remaining costs.

With what was going on in my life at that age, my excitement about going to California for camp was much more social than spiritual.

Cali? I thought. *Cool place to hang. I'm there!*

Outgoing like my dad, I didn't take long to make friends. I was meeting people from different states, including some who had driven cross-country from Pennsylvania to California.

It also didn't take long for the spiritual purpose of the camp to overtake the social aspects, though.

In the camp's first night service, I looked around to see others lifting their hands in worship. I had seen adults, including my parents, praising Jesus like that, but few others my age. It hit me that I was among teenagers who really loved Jesus and had strong relationships with Him. I admitted to myself that I did not have what they had.

What have I been doing? I asked myself. *What have I been missing out on?*

A sense of shame came over me. I thought of all the wrong I had been doing—and had recognized as being wrong—but had chosen not to walk away from. It was the strongest tug toward God's side that I had felt on the tug-of-war rope in my life. I wanted to feel what those around me were obviously feeling.

Jon Courson, now pastor of Applegate Christian Fellowship in Oregon and a well-known Bible commentator, was the special speaker. That first night, he said he was going to teach from Revelation. Hearing a sermon is coming from Revelation, of course, can immediately put a slight scare into an audience. But Courson spoke about "giving all of ourselves to God," and he did so in a way that wasn't scary but full of God's love and mercy. The way his message came across to me was not as a critical "You're a bad person." Instead, it was an encouraging "God has so much more for you."

As I listened, I pictured myself as having reached a cliff in my life. I had two choices: I could take one more step toward rebellion and fall off a cliff, or I could embrace the truth that God loved me and had a plan specifically for me and then surrender my heart to Him.

I felt like God put these words into my heart: "I want to use you, but you are teetering on the edge. You need to run—run away from the lure of the world and run back to Me. I'm right here, waiting for you."

I recommitted my life to God that night. In all my ways, I wanted to pursue Him instead of trying to be cool and popular, and I wanted to stop chasing after the worldly pleasures that hadn't turned out to be nearly as rewarding as I had expected.

After the service, I called my parents and told them about my decision. "My eyes are open," I told them, "and I want to serve Him."

I was so excited that I couldn't fall asleep that night. I lay in my bunk bed in our dorm room and reminisced about my life. Not until that night had I realized just how much heaviness I had been carrying on my shoulders. But all of a sudden, that load had been lifted. It was like going for a run that refreshes you and increases your energy level even though you have just physically exerted yourself. The tug-of-war felt like it had finally come to an end. I stood completely on the side of truth, no longer trying to pull against what I knew was right.

I felt free, no longer in bondage to sin. When we are in sin, we mistake sin for freedom because we can do whatever we want. But we're wrong. Despite how that lifestyle can seem for a while, it is not freedom. It's bondage—bondage to sin.

We can often recognize people who are into alcohol and drugs because the evidence shows on their bodies and faces. They don't look peaceful. Sin places a burden on us, and that night I realized just how much of a burden I had been carrying. I felt "healthy" again.

During praise and worship the next night, I lifted my hands high just like the others. I was experiencing what they possessed—and it didn't take long to understand that I had been missing out on an experience worth pursuing with all my heart.

The Bible studies and the services the rest of the week came alive to me. Courson continued teaching from Revelation, emphasizing how the church could wander away from God's will and the importance of Christians being pure in all their words, actions, and motives. Time after time as he spoke, I thought, *Oh, that's me. Are you talking directly to me?*

One passage we studied dealt with the church in Laodicea. Of the seven churches addressed early in Revelation, that one had become lukewarm. The Laodicean church had been going through its own tug-of-war between doing God's will and pursuing its own worldly pleasures. As a result, the church was hung up in the middle between the two sides, a lifestyle that made the church so unappealing to the Lord that He uttered these words in Revelation 3:16: "So then, because you are lukewarm, and neither cold nor hot, I will vomit you out of My mouth" (NKJV).

That's not exactly the most pleasing word picture in Scripture, but the not-really-hot and not-really-cold church had become so ineffective that it was of no use to God's kingdom. The thought of the

Lord vomiting out the lukewarm Laodiceans snatched my attention, because I had been lukewarm toward Him for the past few years. I had been of no use to His kingdom.

That verse sounded like a warning to me, yet it was a warning issued with love. Yes, I had been messing up. I knew that. I knew that even when I had been doing wrong. But the tone with which the message was delivered caused me to gain an understanding of how much God loved me. He was warning me because He loved me and because He wanted the best for me. Along with that, I realized, He wanted the best of me.

Suddenly all my previous pursuits seemed so empty. It was as though a giant reset button was being pushed in my life and I was embarking on an entirely new way of living.

My conversations with others during the rest of the camp centered less on what states we came from and more on what spiritual states we were in. I recall one conversation with a friend from our youth group during which we talked about returning home and becoming examples for others in our group.

"Let's do this right," we said. "Let's serve the Lord."

Chapter 4

THE CALL

I returned from camp a changed young man. I confessed to my parents about my partying and drinking. Right before we left for camp, the father of a close friend of mine had found alcohol in my friend's pickup. When my parents had learned about that, they wondered if I was drinking, too, but because of the camp they hadn't had an opportunity to confront me and ask.

"We suspected you might be doing something like that," my parents told me when I was back home, "but we're glad the Lord's working on your heart."

Because of my rededication decision at camp, my heart was right with the Lord. But it remained at the center of a battle.

I started really digging into the Bible, and God's Word took on meaning to me in ways it never had before. Studying Scripture with the sense of freedom I enjoyed made it seem like I had previously read the Bible with a veil over my eyes. But with that veil lifted, the words jumped off the pages like crazy and into my heart.

Yet despite my change, I knew there would be struggles in turning completely away from my old ways.

As the summer wound down, I felt an anxiety about returning

to my high school, McCutcheon High, where I had become a cool, popular participant in the party scene. My old friends would be there, and along with them would be the temptation to return to my partying ways. I sensed God telling me, "You're not ready yet." I wasn't the person I am now—very bold and direct about sharing in love that Jesus Christ is my Lord and Savior. With all the insecurities I felt as a teenager, I easily could have been swayed. The church in Crawfordsville whose youth group I attended had a very small school, Maranatha Christian School, and I thought it would offer me the shelter I needed at that stage of my renewed walk in Christ. Of course, attending private school would cost a lot of money. Although our family's financial situation had improved, my parents told me there was no way they could afford to send me to Maranatha, even though they would have made whatever sacrifices they could to make that possible.

I called the school and asked if it would be possible to work there to pay off my tuition. "I'll be a janitor or anything else you need," I offered. School officials said they would allow me to do that.

The next hurdle was how I would get to school because we didn't have an extra car for me to drive to Crawfordsville. But a pastor who spent a lot of time in Ukraine had a car he used only when he was home during the summer, and he offered to let me use his car while he was away.

My parents—probably mostly my dad by that point—weren't convinced, however, that it would work out for me to attend the school.

"Trust me, I can't go to my old high school this year," I told my parents.

My dad had been excited about the coming football season because I was going to be the starting running back for the McCutcheon Mavericks and we were expected to have a very good team. He kept trying to convince me that being on the football team would give me a great platform from which I could tell all the players about my becoming a Christian.

"I'm not a leader, though," I told my dad. "I know I'm not a leader."

But despite my pleas, I was headed to McCutcheon.

The first day of school I flat-out did not want to go. Even getting dressed was a real chore for me. I was afraid that if I walked into the school's hallways again, I would walk away from the Lord.

My mom and I sat in the living room while I reluctantly waited for the bus. My dad, who had been taking a shower, came into the room.

"Jeremy," he said, "the Lord just spoke to me in the shower. He told me that if you are saying that you can't do this, and that He has spoken to you that you need to go to Maranatha, then I need to let you do that."

My mom was thrilled because she said going to Maranatha had been in her heart for me. My parents enrolled me that same day.

It's difficult to explain why, but I just knew that I was supposed to go to that school, that it was part of God's plan for me. With God providing a way for me to go to Maranatha—not to mention a way for me to get there with the loaner car—being admitted into the school was a Jeremiah 29:11 moment for me: "'For I know the plans I have for you,' declares the LORD, 'plans to prosper you and not to harm you, plans to give you hope and a future.'"

I stayed after school an hour each day and cleaned toilets and vacuumed floors. I think I was a pretty good janitor, especially for a teenage boy! I took pride in my job and really wanted the toilets and floors to look clean.

I learned from scrubbing and vacuuming that if God calls you somewhere, you do whatever you can do to fulfill that calling. I would have done whatever was necessary to attend that school.

When I had been asked if I would clean toilets, I answered, "Absolutely."

The example of faith and commitment my dad set was reflected in my answer. The church he started was small at first and not in a position financially to pay him a full-time salary. He still, of course, had to work full-time hours for the church. There was my dad, with four kids at home to provide for, pastoring an infant church that God had led him to start, and to make ends meet he had to take a job with a pizza shop making and delivering pizzas. I knew that had to be a humbling role for my dad, but he never allowed it to become humiliating work.

My daily hour of cleaning commodes and floors was humbling duty, but I never felt embarrassed or humiliated as I had with the car stories I shared earlier. The difference was that I was serving God now, and, as a result, my entire perception of life had changed. When I was younger, I had struggled with insecurity because I was trying to find my security in things. But when I began serving God with all my heart, my security was in Him.

My thinking was, *Man, Jesus loves me. I'm going to serve Him completely. So I'll do whatever it takes. Yeah, I'll wipe down toilets. I don't care.*

Carrying around a scrub brush and pushing a vacuum cleaner, I had never felt securer.

Goodbye to the Gridiron

Changing schools removed me from the party scene I no longer wanted to be associated with. Yet it also took me out of football, and that was difficult for me.

I had a realistic goal of playing football beyond high school. I had played football, baseball, and basketball growing up. I had excelled in baseball, which I began playing at age five. My freshman year, however, I contracted mononucleosis. When I returned to the baseball team, the coach told me, "You have to make up your missed days by running."

Aware that the mono could return if I overexerted myself too soon,

I said I was concerned I might get sick again if I did all that running. "Sorry," the coach answered, "it's not fair to everybody else who was here running and working out every day." So I quit baseball. I hit a good growth spurt before baseball season my sophomore year, and the coach wanted me to come out for the team again. That was during the period when I was too cool for my own good, and I told the coach I wasn't interested in playing on his team. As if my not playing baseball was going to teach him a lesson.

Plus, with my recent growth, football had begun working its way to most-favored status on my sports list. I had started playing football in sixth grade. My sophomore year, I really started playing well. I was a running back and a linebacker, and I was fast, strong, and knew how to run with the ball. During that season, I started thinking football could become my route to college.

When I decided not to return to the public school for my junior year, I went to inform the football coach. "I can't do this," I told him. "I can't come to this school."

A shocked look came across his face. "Why not?" he asked. "You're a starter."

"God's changed my heart," I told him, "and I've got to get away from this."

He didn't seem to fully understand my explanation, but I made clear that my decision was final.

"Okay," he said.

I said the Christian school was "very small." Perhaps I should have said "very, very small." Best I can recall, there were six of us in the high school. Needless to say, the school didn't have a football team or any other sports teams.

Although I was relieved to be out of the public school, I terribly missed playing football.

My dad and I sometimes would drive over to Purdue University in West Lafayette and play worship songs in a small square on campus.

Students would stop and listen for a bit, and sometimes our music created an opportunity for us to share about Christ with them.

One Friday night we were driving over to Purdue when we drove right past my old high school. The lights of the football stadium were shining bright, and I could see into the stadium enough to see the fans in the stands and the players on the field.

I started weeping right there in the passenger seat of my dad's car.

My dad knew how badly I missed football, and when he saw the tears on my face, he reached over and placed his hand on my back. "Jeremy," he said, "you're doing what the Lord has called you to do. And I'm proud of you."

Even today, remembering how I felt driving past the game and then my dad's words still makes me want to cry. That was a powerful moment.

Walking away from football that year was a big turning point in my life. After a few years of doing my own thing, I was putting aside my own dreams and desires to do what God wanted me to do. That wasn't easy. Even now as an adult, it can be difficult to do. But to truly serve the Lord, we have to be willing to give up things that we truly love if they are not in line with God's will for our lives. In my case there wasn't anything wrong with playing football. It wasn't a bad thing; it was a good thing. But as I can reflect from a place a couple of decades further down the path God prepared, He had a much better thing than football in store for me.

Without sports to play at my new school, I began spending more time with music. Some friends and I formed a garage band. We played cover songs, although the bands we were covering probably would not have been too proud if they could have heard us perform. I can't remember the name of our band, but I do recall that when things weren't going well for us, we changed our name to Temple Rising. We didn't change anything about the band, just our name. That didn't fix the reason we hadn't been doing well.

My listening interests ranged from Christian recording artists such as Steven Curtis Chapman to many different rock bands. Occasionally, my musical choices demonstrated that, although I had come a long way since my partying days, I still had cravings that weren't in my best interest. I don't want to come across as saying all music that isn't Christian is bad. That's not the case. But the problem for me was the attitude behind my listening choices. I hadn't completely washed away all my rebellious nature. I still had moments when I wanted to prove that I could be my own person and do the things that I wanted to do.

During that time of musical exploration, I began to understand more about music and sampled other forms, including a little funk and a little reggae. Lyrics aside, because I was self-taught and able to play by ear, I picked up a diverse influence musically.

But while my listening choices were varied, I began writing songs for our band to play that had a narrow focus: my blossoming faith in Jesus. Our music became a way to express what was taking place within my heart, and gradually my heart was moving more and more toward music.

Seeing the Light

By the end of my junior year in the Christian school, I was feeling an urge to return to McCutcheon to finish high school. I wanted to play football and also put into use what I had learned spiritually.

I knew returning to public school would be a challenge, but I wanted that challenge to see where I stood spiritually. I felt I was strong enough spiritually, but I still had some of the fears I had when I had chosen to transfer to Maranatha.

I desperately wanted to play football, but at the same time I didn't want to spend an entire school year at McCutcheon. The solution was to take a loaded schedule that would allow me to graduate at the Christmas break.

Football season didn't pan out as I had hoped.

For one, although I still loved football, I just wasn't into it as much as I had been. Before the camp in California, football had been my life. Now serving God was my life. Also, the year off from football made achieving my goal of playing in college much more difficult. Because I hadn't played as a junior, I had missed out on the most important year for being noticed by college recruiters.

I played full-time on defense, but I wound up only splitting time at my favorite position, running back. Our team had not been expected to do well that season. Because of that, the coaches wanted to give part of the carries to a sophomore running back so that he could gain experience for when the team was expected to improve in the next couple of seasons. The coaches said that because I hadn't played the previous season, I needed to prove myself. But being in a situation where opportunities to carry the ball were split between the running backs made it difficult to prove myself to the coaches. I had friends who wanted me to be the full-time running back, and they would sit in the stands at home games and chant, "Give Camp the ball! Give Camp the ball!" My dad became so frustrated that after one game he politely asked to speak with the coach.

"Is Jeremy faster than the other running back?" my dad asked the coach.

"Yes," the coach replied.

"Is Jeremy stronger?"

"Yes."

"Is Jeremy a better runner overall?"

"Oh yeah."

"Then why don't you put him in more?" my dad concluded. "Is it politics?"

"It's not," the coach replied.

Going to my coach like that was so atypical of my dad, but that was an irritating time for us because my goal was to go to Purdue and walk on—play initially without a scholarship in hopes of earning one for future seasons—and having a big senior season at running back in one of the local high schools would have helped my chances of doing so. But I can look back now and see my senior season as the Lord saying, "This is not what I have for you." The Lord just had different plans for me from what I had for myself.

The half year I spent at McCutcheon indeed was a challenge. I still had some of the same cravings for worldly pleasures that I had before rededicating my life to Christ. I didn't go out drinking and partying like before, but I did battle those desires in my mind. My old friends were still partying, but I had decided not to hang out with them. Although we were in the same classes and hallways, it felt like we were in such different worlds.

I didn't know any real Christians at our school, and part of the reason was that I wasn't bold about saying "I'm a Christian now." I was still trying to be cool, and because of the cravings I still possessed, I wrongly believed I wasn't worthy enough to be bold for Christ.

After high school, when I became bolder with my witness and because of my music career became known as a Christian, I would come across former classmates who would tell me, "Hey, I was a Christian back then too." I look back now and ask myself, *What was I doing?* I could have made such an impact if I had gone back to that school my senior year, stood up, and been bold for Christ. Assertiveness now guides my heart with today's youth, especially those who have had a spiritual transformation and who God has really done a work in. I encourage them to get into their high schools and lead a charge for change.

Matthew 5:14–16 says, "You are the light of the world. A town built on a hill cannot be hidden. Neither do people light a lamp and put it under a bowl. Instead they put it on its stand, and it gives light to everyone in the house. In the same way, let your light shine before others, that they may see your good deeds and glorify your Father in heaven."

I tell teens to think about being in a big, dark room where one person with a light pops up. And then someone sees that light and pops up with his or her light. Then more and more people with lights pop up until their lights have overtaken the darkness.

But until one person stands and uncovers his or her light, the room remains covered in darkness, like at my school. I didn't stand up and make my light seen, and I didn't know of anyone else who did, either. Light always pierces darkness, and sometimes all it takes is one bold person to completely change an entire room.

Time to Cut Ties

After finishing my senior year early, I spent the spring working on a custom-blinds assembly line at the Lafayette Venetian Blind company and struggling to decide what I would do next: go to Purdue, study business management or accounting, and try to play football; or attend Calvary Chapel Bible College in California.

I now recognize that as another tug-of-war between what God had planned for me and my selfish desires, and I had a difficult time determining in which direction I should go. I kept going back and forth.

My parents could have pushed me to attend Bible college, and they could have pulled me to stay close to home at Purdue. They did neither. They weren't bugging me by asking, "What are you going to do with your life?" Instead, they focused on what I was doing at the time: helping at their church, leading worship sometimes, and taking part in Bible studies.

"Just serve the Lord," they would say. "You have a job, and you're serving the Lord." That is the wisdom my parents possess. My focus was on trying to figure out what God wanted me to do next. Their focus was on what I was doing for God at the moment, knowing that as I continued to serve Him, He would reveal to me what He wanted me to do next.

One night I had a dream in which I walked into a room of our house where my mom was on the telephone. She hung up the phone.

"Who was that?" I asked.

"It was Satan," she answered, not alarmed at all, speaking matter-of-factly. "Do you have his number?"

"Yeah," I said.

I awakened in a cold sweat. I had no idea what the dream meant, but it frightened me that Satan was in it. I did not have the dream again, but it didn't leave my mind for two weeks. I knew the dream had a meaning, but I didn't know what it was until God put it on my heart: I still had Satan's phone number because I had not completely cut all ties with him. It was time for me to move on and never look back. *I have a plan for you*, I sensed God speaking to me, *and I want you to dig into My Word.*

That was it, the answer was crystal clear: God's will was for me to go to Bible college.

Chapter 5

HEADING WEST

A T-shirt helped make it possible for me to move to California for college. When my dad became a Christian, the Holy Spirit transformed his life immediately and radically. After he sobered up the night he was saved at the Assemblies of God church, he was done with alcohol for good. Just like that.

My dad's outgoing personality didn't change, but when combined with his changed heart, he began to point people in a different direction. My dad loved Jesus and sought out any opportunity to tell people about Him.

My dad went to a gym one day wearing one of those "God's Gym" T-shirts that played off the Gold's Gym logo. I remember that some people considered the God's Gym shirts a little cheesy, but my dad wasn't overly concerned with what people thought about his clothing.

Sure enough, a man in the gym came over to my dad and said, "I like your shirt."

The man introduced himself as Keith March, a doctor, and the two hit it off because he liked my dad's boldness with his faith. They became friends, and Dr. March wound up helping our family and church through the years.

One time, when Dr. March learned we didn't have any type of stereo system in our home, he bought us a CD player. He also took our family with his to a Newsboys concert, and he paid for my dad and me to go with him and his son to a Promise Keepers event in Colorado. He helped our church meet different needs too. Observing Dr. March's heartfelt generosity really impacted that season of my life.

When Dr. March learned I wanted to attend Bible college, he said he would pay for my first semester. I was blown away. Calvary Chapel Bible College (CCBC) had a different setup from the typical college. Private universities can be very expensive, and Calvary Chapel was structured in a way that it could keep costs as low as possible.

First, the school had a two-year degree program. (It has since added four-year degrees.) Second, it wasn't an accredited university, which allowed the school to hire pastors who might not have had the degrees required to teach at an accredited university but still had the experience and knowledge to train students for ministry.

Even though the cost would be less compared with other Bible colleges, I still knew it was going to take a combination of God's provision and my hard work to pay for college. I had saved what I could from my job making venetian blinds and other previous jobs, but it wasn't much. I knew I was going to have to work my way through college.

Dr. March funding my first semester allowed me to start college pressure-free financially and also to begin setting aside money for future semesters from my jobs while in California. Dr. March was yet another blessing God placed into my life and my family.

I started Bible college in the fall of 1996, and I was so excited to be there. Going into a Christian college environment was important for me because I believed I needed time to separate myself from the worldly pleasures I had been around during high school.

Psalm 24:4 describes the person who may stand in the holy place of the Lord as "the one who has clean hands and a pure heart, who does not trust in an idol or swear by a false god." That clean-handed and pure-hearted person is who I wanted to be, a difference-maker so in pursuit of God that I could not be distracted by my own desires or worldly pleasures.

I felt sure that I had been called into ministry, although I did not know what type. I enjoyed playing the guitar and leading worship in my dad's church, and writing songs every now and then provided both a creative outlet and an avenue for expressing my feelings and my faith. But I wasn't yet thinking along the lines of music being my ministry.

I did know that I wanted to dig deeper into God's Word. I didn't want to merely read scriptures and say, "That was cool." I wanted to comprehend what I was reading. I wanted to take a section, study it, and say, "Okay, I know this much right now. Now I'm going to sit on this for a little bit and ask, 'What is this passage really doing in my heart?'"

Truly experiencing a life-changing faith in Jesus means taking His Word off the pages of the Bible and allowing it to sink into our hearts so that it directs our actions.

So I would read and ask, "What are You saying, Lord?" Sometimes, I would pray, "What do You mean by this?" Then I would meditate on the passage. I wanted to act out Philippians 4:8, which says, "Finally, brothers and sisters, whatever is true, whatever is noble, whatever is right, whatever is pure, whatever is lovely, whatever is admirable—if anything is excellent or praiseworthy—think about such things."

If a thought didn't meet the apostle Paul's checklist, I didn't want to grant it priority in my mind.

Then I wanted to take the next step of living out what Scripture says. God's Word is living and active.[2] When we truly study it and meditate on it, it does something within us. I chose a simple plan: open my Bible to Genesis and work my way through Revelation. CCBC had a strong emphasis on Bible classes. Right from the start of my first semester, I knew I needed the in-depth study in the classroom to go with what I desired to learn in my private devotional time. I was a sponge in my classes.

Digging In

Less than a month in, I experienced a monumental moment. We were studying the gospel of John, and the professor, Pastor Chuck Wooley, was talking about Jesus and His love, and the need to be set apart and have our hearts cleansed.

Pastor Wooley was an amazing teacher as it was, but the more he talked about cleansing our hearts, the more my emotions began to build up within me. I was so hungry spiritually, and I needed that cleansing he was talking about.

It was a night class, the last session of the day. CCBC's campus is now in Murrieta, California. But during my first semester, the school moved there from Big Bear, California, a beautiful area in the mountains northeast of San Bernardino. Up in the mountains I could take a deep breath and soak in the soothing aroma of the pine trees all around.

The campus was small—there were about five hundred students—and the sanctuary was in a retreat center that had a lodge-like feel to it. I picked a spot in the back, sat down, and began to weep. I cried for almost two hours straight, with my head buried in my hands most of that time.

I had to be a sight. I wasn't sitting in a chair; I was sitting on the top of the back of a chair with my feet on the cushioned seat part. I was stout looking from my workouts, and given the small number of students, it was pretty well known that I had come to California from Indiana. I had long hair in a ponytail then, and I shaved the sides of my head.

Needless to say, I stuck out to begin with at CCBC. Here was this burly, outgoing, Midwestern dude with the crazy hairstyle, just weeping and weeping and weeping.

There were other students in the sanctuary, but I didn't care. When someone would ask if I was okay, I'd look up and say, "God's dealing with me," then I'd put my head back in my hands and continue to cry.

In his book, the prophet Ezekiel discussed a time when God would give the people of Israel a new heart and place a new spirit within them.[3] When the tears stopped and I began to reflect on what had just taken place on the back of that seat, I felt that God had given me a new heart and placed a new spirit within me.

It's not that there had been anything woefully evil about my heart. I was a Christian, living like one, and seeking to develop an even closer relationship with Christ. But there still was a lot of junk in my heart.

The best way I can describe what took place would be to compare my heart with a closet that needs a thorough cleaning. You take inventory of what should be in the closet, and then you throw out some things or rearrange the items you need to keep. You tidy up the floor so that you can actually walk into your closet again. When the job is finished, you're tired because you are fully aware you've been through a major overhaul, but it's all worthwhile when you stand at the entrance and behold what looks like a brand-new closet.

I hoped that's the way God felt when He looked at my heart as I walked away from that seat. I knew for sure, though, that I felt good about what had taken place. So much junk had been removed. I had grown tired of all that junk still lingering around. I hated it, in fact. I had wanted to be set apart, but my inability to throw out all those selfish desires had become an obstacle.

From that point on, I was pedal to the metal for God.

One of the changes I noticed right away was the compassion I felt toward others. I had always been respectful of others and nice to them because that's what my parents had raised me to do. Being nice and respectful, though, falls well short of having a heart that aches for others. The heart that aches for others comes from having compassion. When we allow Christ to let us see others the way that He sees them, we notice more situations around us where the hope of Christ is needed. We don't merely feel for those people, we feel compassion for them.

It wasn't as though I needed to change so people would like me or want to be around me. It was that I needed to change so that God could work through me like I wanted Him to—and like He wanted to. It wasn't that I needed to change so I could benefit. It was that I needed to change so others could benefit—and God could be glorified.

My love for others increased seemingly exponentially.

I would see someone sitting on a bench around campus who looked depressed or anguished, and my heart would begin to ache for that person. I would feel a pull within my spirit to go over and tell that person that Jesus loved him, that there was hope in Christ, and that Jesus had so much in store He wanted to give to him. It became a personal mission to share Jesus' love and hope with others. And that mission didn't grow from mere knowledge that I had learned in a classroom—I had experienced His presence myself on my own lonely seat.

The next time I was back home in Indiana, I apologized to my brother Jared and asked his forgiveness for not being a better brother. Jared was eight years younger than me, and the age difference probably kept us from being as close to each other as we could have been. Plus, we had opposite personalities. He was more reserved, like my mom. I was more let's-do-something-crazy, like my dad.

When my sensitivity toward others increased, I realized that I had not been the exemplary big brother for Jared that I should have been. When I asked his forgiveness, Jared graciously replied, "Oh, you're fine." (He got that trait from my mom too.) But I knew better. I knew I had missed out on opportunities to be the close big brother he needed and to make a positive impact on his life.

At college I felt closer to Jesus than ever before. My times of worship—both as an individual and with the student body—were amazing. During chapel services, the worship reminded me of the power I sensed during the first night of that summer camp. Except now

I was an active part of that worship experience, not a witness. We had great conversations around campus. We shared needs with one another and prayed together. We did a lot of celebrating about what God was doing in our lives because we had a deep interest in one another. We learned about one another's upbringings and spiritual journeys.

Our student body included a wide variety of backgrounds, from new Christians full of zeal and passion to the more seasoned ones who already had a strong knowledge of Scripture. With all those different walks of life coming together, and the different perspectives we brought with us, we asked difficult questions about God's Word and really dug into the meaning of scriptures. As I learned more about my fellow students, I felt like I was able to walk through every gamut of life with them.

During my alone time, I would go off to a part of a mountain, pray, and sing words of worship to the Lord: "Thank You, Lord" or "Praise You, Lord." I felt like I was hanging out with Jesus!

Learning to Lead

To borrow from Jesus' parable about the wise and foolish builders,[4] I would describe my foundation when I started attending CCBC as part rock and part sand. I believe that unstable foundation is one reason why I didn't think I was prepared to go back to my public school after my recommitment at summer camp.

The Bible classes at CCBC definitely solidified my foundation. We studied through most of the books of the Bible, and we really expounded on books that were deep in theology, such as Hebrews, Romans, and Isaiah, to name a few. On top of our professors' instruction, we also listened to what we called "Chuck tapes." Pastor Chuck Smith, who started the Calvary Chapel movement, was a phenomenal teacher of the Word, and we listened to tapes of him teaching verse by verse. I took detailed notes on what I was learning from Scripture in the classroom, and during my individual Bible study, I highlighted texts, underlined key words, and wrote notes in the margins. Section by section, I was establishing a solid and complete foundation on which to build the rest of my life.

Musically, I would play guitar and sing in my room or sometimes in the school cafeteria, but music still wasn't an area of ministry I was considering. I truly was all about learning God's Word. One day I was playing around with a guitar in the cafeteria when someone asked, "Do you play?"

"Yeah."

"Play a song," he said.

I did, and when I finished, he said, "Oh, wow."

Another person came up to me and said, "You should lead worship in chapel."

"Yeah," I said. "I'd love to."

I was so nervous the first time I led worship in chapel. Leading worship is like watching a game show on television: it looks so easy until you are the one doing it. I'm outgoing and comfortable on a stage now, but I was super shy my first time in front of a chapel service. I was so concerned about coming across as arrogant that I went to the other extreme. I was worshipping, but in a very introverted way.

But still, during my first time to lead worship at CCBC, I thought, *Wow, I'm enjoying this!*

I had led worship in my dad's church and at Bible studies back home, but my heart had become so different since then that for the first time I felt like I was ministering or truly using a gift for the Lord, and that I was being used by Him. I was stoked!

That first time in chapel led to me leading worship twice a week at CCBC, and then came invitations to lead worship or sing a couple of songs in area churches. I would get nervous each time because I was afraid of messing up.

Honestly, although I had led worship in Indiana, I didn't really understand how to be a worship leader. I can't remember how long this learning curve took, but I reached a point where I said to myself, *Hey, just do what you do when you're in the audience, but you're going to be the one leading instead.*

I learned that a worship leader leads by worshipping. If as the leader you're most concerned about making sure the people in the audience are okay, then you're missing out on the fullness of the depth of the worship time. I decided that when I led, I was going to worship Jesus. And that's what I did, and the others worshipped Jesus with me. It was an amazing experience to worship in a manner that led others into worship.

I didn't have my own guitar, so whenever I would lead, sing in a church, or play during my alone time, I would have to bum one off a friend.

After Dr. March covered my first semester, I paid for the second semester by stocking office supplies at Staples. The summer after my second semester, I took a construction job that helped pay for my third semester. It was all I could do to pay for school, so purchasing a guitar was out of the question.

I wasn't even sure I was going to be able to finish my two years because I didn't have enough money for my fourth semester. But because I had been working every semester and during the summer, the school worked out a payment plan with me that would allow me to attend my final semester, then receive my degree when I had paid off all the tuition and fees.

The opportunities to minister through music continued to increase. Students would pass along invitations to me to sing at their churches with their youth groups or in their main services. I also was in a band with some other students, and we led worship and put on concerts at school every once in a while. That allowed us to perform songs we each had written.

Back then I never consciously decided to write a song, to then sit down and write it. My songs came from my relationship with the Lord, based on something He had done in my heart or something I had read that caused me to reflect on Him. What's cool is I can look back on the lyrics I wrote and see how God was speaking to me. In one song called "Looking Back," the chorus says,

> The cross on which You've hung
> Is not a place for a king to be
> Lord, the wounds that stung, You did it all for,
> You did it all for me.

That song came out of a time when I wanted to get out of my own selfishness and not take for granted the fact that Jesus Christ had given His own life for me. My writing became like a self-feeding cycle in which I would write what I was reflecting on, and then that would allow me to reflect even further on what I was writing. It was like the deepening of my relationship with the Lord was leading me to go even deeper with Him.

Chapter 6

THE GIFT

When I finished school, I decided to stay in California and continue working as a bagger at Vons grocery store to pay off my school debt. Toward the end of the summer, my friends and I decided to break up the band we had put together, so I started spending a lot of time hanging out with musical friends from the College and Career ministry at Calvary Chapel Vista, near San Diego, about half an hour away from CCBC. We would get together and jam, and I also was helping lead worship for our College and Career services.

That fall Jean-Luc Lajoie of The Kry came to our area looking for musicians to fill a youth band he wanted to form for Harvest Crusades. Someone had recommended that Jean-Luc check me out, so he came one night to listen to us practice.

Afterward, Jean-Luc talked to me a few minutes, said he liked a song we played that I had written, offered a few observations he had made of me, and then told me about his youth band plans. He said he would be interested in talking to me about my interest in joining the band and suggested we both pray about it and get back together to talk more.

I liked Jean-Luc right off the bat, and we started hanging out a little. He obviously had a deep love for Jesus, and despite how popular The Kry was—they were well known nationally, but they were *the* band in California at the time—he was a really down-to-earth dude. When Jean-Luc's plans for forming the youth band progressed, he invited me to join. I told Jean-Luc I would pray about it.

Those early days of uncertainty after college bore some similarities to when I was trying to decide whether to go to Bible college or try to play football at Purdue. But there was one notable difference. Before, my choice basically boiled down to God's will (Bible college) or my will (football). This time, my options all had to do with ministry. There wasn't a clear-cut, God's-way-or-my-way conflict.

My dad's church in Lafayette was five years old by that point, and he told me how much he would love for me to return home and work alongside him leading worship. But he also encouraged me to seek God's will for my life, and if God wanted me somewhere other than his church, then that was what he wanted for me too.

At one point during that time, I wondered if I was missing out on something. I was watching a college football game on TV one Saturday afternoon. The player who had been expected to be my backup running back if I had played my junior year in high school was playing in the game, and he scored a touchdown and rushed for more than a hundred yards. He was playing great in a nationally televised football game while I was working at a grocery store and, although I had a couple of options involving music, not really playing music yet.

That could have been me playing football on TV, I thought.

But then I remembered my dad's words on the Friday night three years earlier when we had driven past the high school football game I could have been playing in: "You're doing what the Lord has called you to do."

Shortly after watching my former teammate in the TV game, I had the opportunity to play and sing at a camp. The amount on the check the camp gave me was larger than any check I had received for playing music. It also just so happened to be large enough to pay off what I owed to CCBC. With the school debt paid off, I quit my job at Vons in December 1998, moved out of the place where I had been staying with a friend and his grandparents in Oceanside, and went back to Indiana unsure whether I would stay home for good or return to California.

At a major crossroads in my life, I had serious conversations with my parents about the options I had and my search for God's will for me. As usual, my mom pointed me to scriptures that spoke to what I was going through. My dad knew the importance of the decision I was facing, so he suggested the two of us go stay at a friend's cabin where we could fast and pray for a few days.

That was a special time with my dad. There was no media in the cabin. We didn't have cell phones. We fasted and prayed together, and we spent time fishing and just talking. I remember having such a soothing peace while we were there. In my prayer time, I told God I didn't want to reexperience my tugs-of-war of old. I didn't want to do my own thing as I had previously. I told God whatever He wanted me to do, I would do.

While we were at the cabin, I felt God speaking to my heart that He wanted me to go back to the West Coast.

Are You sure? I asked Him. *I moved out of my place. I am ready to serve here at Harvest. Do You really want a jobless, homeless dude heading back to California?*

In my quiet time, I felt a strong affirmation that it was God's will for me to return to California. I believed God had a plan and would give me everything I needed to follow His leading.

Telling my dad wasn't easy. On the car ride home, I broke the news to him.

I know my choice had to be crushing for my dad. I can imagine how exciting it would be for a father to have his son join him in ministry, but that wasn't going to happen. I apologized to him, and he said he understood.

After we were home, I had one more sit-down talk with my parents about my decision. They both agreed that I was doing the right thing.

Christmas to Remember

I stayed in Indiana through Christmas. Our family was together on Christmas morning, with April and her husband, Trent, joining us. Every Christmas morning, our parents would pick one of us kids to pass out the presents, and that year I was the designated distributor.

I handed out all the gifts except for the biggest one, which had been tucked behind the tree. There was no name tag on the wrapping.

"Whose is this?" I asked.

"That's yours," my mom said.

I had no idea what it was, but I started unwrapping. I noticed everyone had stopped what they were doing to watch me.

As I tore the paper off, I could see from the box it was a guitar. And not just any guitar, but a Taylor brand guitar, which I knew carried a price tag of about $2,000!

I was completely shocked. Not only had I never asked for a Taylor, but I also had never allowed myself to even dream of getting one. To ask for one would have been asking for something twenty times greater than my biggest gift ever, so opening up a guitar was more than I could dream of.

Tears filled my eyes, and others in the room were crying too. I looked over my gift, still in disbelief, and I remember clearly the words that came to my mind: *Lord, whatever You want. Not my plans but Yours. Here I am.*

A sense of anticipation came over my heart as I started to play my new instrument. Although I hadn't been thinking I could become a full-time musician, I had begun to realize that God had given me the gift of musical abilities. My parents' gift was a strong affirmation that music was a gift to be completely turned over to God. And now I wouldn't have to ask a friend to borrow his guitar to use that gift!

Before Christmas, I had told my mom that I really needed a guitar. Jean-Luc had told me I had to get one because I was the only person he knew who borrowed guitars to play in churches. But I told my mom I had no idea how I'd ever be able to afford one.

"I know, I know," my mom said, hiding the fact that she and my dad had already purchased one.

My parents knew from our phone conversations how much I enjoyed leading worship at school and in churches. They sensed that God was using music to work in and through my life.

One day when my mom was washing dishes, she strongly felt like she and my dad needed to buy me a guitar even though they didn't have the money for one. It turned out that my dad had the same impression separately.

So they decided to take out a loan to purchase the Taylor. They considered it an investment in my spiritual future. But before signing for the loan, they asked my sister and brothers to sign off on giving me a guitar. They explained to April, Jared, and Josh that they couldn't afford gifts like that for them, too, and their gifts would be much more inexpensive than mine that year. But my sister and brothers were excited because they knew how much a guitar would mean to me, and they gave my parents their go-ahead for the plan.

For my flight back to California, there was no way I was going to check my most-prized possession as luggage. I carried my baby onto the plane with me.

When I boarded, I could see the overhead bins were beginning to fill. I began to get a little paranoid. I told a flight attendant, "I can't put this anywhere but in the overhead bin." If the airline would have let me, I would have stood in the aisle for the entire flight and put my guitar in my seat—seat belt fastened around it too. The flight attendant was sweet and understanding, and she helped me find a place to carefully stow my treasure.

I landed in California with one bag and my guitar. I didn't have a job, I didn't have a place to live, and I didn't have much of a plan beyond my friend Bryan picking me up at the airport and taking me to a youth pastors' conference at CCBC.

During the youth conference, I bumped into a friend named Isaiah Thompson, whom I had met while attending Calvary Chapel Vista.

"Hey, man, I heard you need a place to stay," Isaiah said. I don't know how he had heard that. (Perhaps my friend at the college whose dorm room I was crashing in was making it known I needed a place!)

"I do," I said.

Isaiah told me that his grandmother in Vista was looking for someone she could give room and board in exchange for looking after her, buying her groceries, taking her to doctors' appointments, and running other errands for her.

I had no other options at that point, so I accepted Grandma Marge's offer through Isaiah.

The next day, my youth pastor, Dave Hole, gave me a ride to her house. When we pulled up to the address Isaiah had given me, I told Dave, "I guess this must be the place."

"You mean you've never been here before?" Dave asked. "You don't know this lady at all?"

"Nope, but I guess this is where I'm gonna stay."

The Next Stage

I knocked on the front door, and a smiling, gray-haired, grandmotherly-type woman answered.

"Hi, Marge? I'm Jeremy," I said. "I guess I'm going to be living with you."

"Oh, you have such beautiful eyes," Grandma Marge said. "Come on in!"

Marge led me to her breakfast nook, where we sat at the table and began introducing ourselves to each other. She asked about me, so I told her about growing up in Indiana, moving to California to attend Bible college, playing music, and going back home before feeling like God wanted me to move back to California—even though I had no place to live.

Marge told me about her husband, who had served in the military and had passed away a few years earlier. She also talked about her faith, and as she told me some of what she had been through in life that had both tested and strengthened her faith, I could sense the resolve in her heart. Our conversation carried a touch of sadness, too, because it was obvious she missed the companionship of her husband. Yet Marge smiled the entire time we talked.

"Let me show you to your room," she said after about an hour. "If you want to go shopping for groceries tomorrow, here's my credit card."

I sat my one bag and my guitar on the bedroom floor. When Marge left, I sat on the bed and took a deep breath. I had needed only one trip to carry everything I owned into my room, and my arms hadn't even been overloaded. I had less than twenty dollars in my bank account. I had a cell phone, but no car.

All right, Lord, I thought. *Here I am. What do You have in mind for me?*

I called Jean-Luc that day to tell him I was in town, and he informed me that the youth band he had wanted to form didn't work out. But because we had hit it off so well when we met, we stayed in touch with each other and hung out some.

One day Jean-Luc called and asked if I wanted to help sell The Kry merchandise at a concert. That night led to more invitations to work the merch table at concerts. Jean-Luc and his brother, Yves, would give me a little money for helping out. Every bit of income meant a lot to me.

More helpful than the money, though, were the relationships that developed with Jean-Luc and Yves. Being around them allowed me to see how much integrity they had on and off the stage.

Jean-Luc would be very direct with me with questions such as "Are you staying in the Word?" and "Have you been praying?" and "What's God shown you lately?" I needed his directness to hold me accountable. I knew Jean-Luc would be asking me those questions, and that anticipation helped me stay disciplined in my spiritual habits.

There was one question he asked a lot that we still ask of each other: "How's your carpet time doing?" We would literally lie on the floor, facedown on the carpet, and pray.

Jean-Luc talked about the Lord all the time. He encouraged me a lot. Because of my uncertainty as I sought what God had in store for me, I needed Jean-Luc's encouragement in addition to his directness.

Jean-Luc also mentored me musically, and—thankfully—he was just as direct with me about my music as he was my spiritual life.

"Oh, buddy," he'd say in his great French-Canadian accent after listening to me, "your timing is not good sometimes." Or "Man, when you're singing, sing what you mean." He would ask, "What are you saying?" to make me think about the message of the words. When I would tell him what I was thinking, he would enthusiastically say, "*Sing it!*" But then he also would be very intentional about encouraging me. He liked to tell me when I played and sang, "Man, I love your heart."

After we'd been hanging together for a while, Jean-Luc asked if I wanted to play a song at their concert that night. I was caught off guard because I hadn't expected that question. I was thrilled just to work the merch table and learn by watching The Kry in action.

"I would *love* to," I said with a big smile.

I was so nervous when I took my place among the band members and looked out at the crowd. I mean, this was *The Kry* I was onstage with. My first song with them was "Get Away." I think I was more concerned with Jean-Luc than with the crowd because he was such a perfectionist musically. Anytime I felt myself getting off rhythm, I would cringe on the inside. I was so fearful of messing up that I felt like a robot onstage as I played.

I called my parents. "Guess what—I got onstage and played a song with The Kry!" I told them. They were excited and asked what it was like.

"It was crazy," I said. "I was so nervous!"

My parents wished they could have been there to see me onstage—even though it was only for one song—and they told me how proud they were of me. My parents were always telling me how proud they were of me. My dad had a certain way of saying it that has always been special, and he told me that during the phone call: "I'm so proud of you because you're serving the Lord." (I still love it when he says that today.)

Either Jean-Luc didn't notice or—more likely—he overlooked that I was about as smooth as C-3PO my first time onstage because he allowed me to play with The Kry a few more times.

It was clear that some type of music ministry was becoming a direction I was moving toward, and people around me were encouraging that. But I wasn't ready to step forward and declare I wanted to be a full-time musician or a music minister. I hadn't had a "This is what I want to do" or an "I want to be this" moment. When pressed about music, I would say, "If that's what God wants, cool." I had set my own path before and witnessed the negative effects that had, and I did not want to do that again. But I did feel like God was opening doors for me in music.

A big door opened when Jean-Luc said, "Hey, why don't you play one of your songs?" At Cedarville College (now University) in Ohio, I performed before The Kry for the first time, singing "This Man" and then played "Get Away" with the band again.

The rush was incredible. After hearing the response of the crowd and feeling how the Lord was in that place and my music as part of people experiencing His presence, I left the stage that night thinking, *This is it—this is what I'm called to do!*

I became driven to play and sing, and to share my heart. More opportunities to do just that came, again thanks to Jean-Luc.

When The Kry would receive concert invitations from local churches for dates it already had booked, Jean-Luc would refer the churches to me.

I had to bum rides or borrow friends' cars to get to the churches until an acquaintance heard of my situation and offered to let me drive an older extra car he wasn't using. It was just like how people had provided cars for my parents when I was growing up. The car I drove wasn't much better looking, either. It was a Nissan Sentra—a 1981 model, I believe—and when I'd hit a bump, the trunk would fly open.

I never put my Taylor guitar in the trunk. A guitar should never, never, never be placed in a trunk anyway, but especially in one that might pop open without notice.

A funny thing about that car was that it was a stick shift, and it was old enough that the numbers had been rubbed off the knob on top of the gear stick. When I got up in speed in fourth gear on the freeways, the engine would rev with an annoying high-pitched whine. A friend riding with me one day suggested above the whine that the car might be a five-speed.

"Where would fifth gear be?" I asked him.

He told me to try to shift all the way over to the right and up. Sure enough—it was a five-speed! The car sounded much better at higher speeds after that discovery.

My Taylor guitar was worth more money than the car, but as my parents had been with the various gift cars they had received, I was grateful that God had placed it on someone's heart to meet my need.

Living at Grandma Marge's kept my expenses low. I wouldn't tell Jean-Luc I was nearly broke, though. The Kry would give me a hundred dollars or so for working the merch table, and I was picking up a little money from singing in churches. That was it for income, but I didn't really have any worries over finances. I had never had much money anyway, so I didn't feel like I was doing without anything I needed.

Those might seem like lean times, but I look back at them as very fruitful times. I was growing spiritually as part of a great College and Career group at Calvary Chapel Vista. Jean-Luc was pouring into me spiritually and musically. Through music, I was seeing God use me and open doors for me. And, finally, I was beginning to feel a specific calling in my life.

Chapter 7

BROKE-UP AND BROKEN

*I*t was a request, like others I was receiving from college friends in the spring of 1999, from Jason Duff, who asked if I would lead worship for a Bible study group he led weekly at Palomar College. A supportive group of friends had been finding music opportunities for me in their churches and small groups. I liked to lead worship any chance I got, and being able to help out a good friend like Jason was a bonus.

Jason told me about one particular student he had met in his Bible study group. "She's amazing," he told me. "You ought to see how much she loves the Lord." I could already see how interested Jason was in her.

Jason introduced me to Melissa Henning when I arrived at Palomar. She had dark brown hair, big ol' brown eyes, and the best smile anyone could hope to see. *Wow*, I thought. *He was right—she is lovely.* Jason definitely seemed to have chosen a good one.

There were about eight students in Jason's Bible study that night, and we formed a circle to start the praise and worship. It was a small group, but it was an awesome time of singing and praising God. All the students were really into it, but one in particular kept catching my attention—Jason's friend Melissa.

I had never seen anyone our age with such unrestrained passion for God. She sang with complete abandon, arms fully outstretched. She was so deep into the Lord's presence that I felt like an outsider. After the Bible study concluded, Melissa and I chatted briefly.

I saw her at the Bible study over the next few weeks and in a few other group settings. Jason kept talking to me about her and how much he thought of her. Jason, though, never said anything that indicated Melissa felt the same way about him. When I observed both of them in the same group, Jason's hope that they would become more than friends appeared one-sided.

In fact, as I was around Melissa more, it seemed the only chemistry that was developing was between her and me.

I called Melissa to tell her what I was noticing about us, and she confirmed that we had a common interest in each other. But we also had something else in common: we were friends with Jason. Actually, Jason was one of my best friends, and I knew that he was really optimistic that something would develop between him and Melissa.

Melissa and I agreed we were in a difficult spot. We didn't want to hurt Jason, but we enjoyed talking with each other so much and we wanted to keep hanging out. We would meet for lunch or coffee and talk about God, music, and a lot of different things. Jason had been right when he said Melissa was amazing. She was just a very happy person—a very joyous person.

Melissa told me she had been raised in a Christian home, but she had strayed a little—nothing bad, but more like not being as committed to God as she thought she needed to be. One day God had spoken to her heart about her straying. She realized what she was doing and recommitted herself to following God. Other members of her family had been traveling a similar path as Melissa, and she helped bring her family back to an all-out commitment to God like she had made. Melissa was a leader and an effective witness, and I admired that about her.

She was so devoted to the Lord. A few of my fun-loving friends and I had a tendency to get a bit silly sometimes during Bible study meetings. I was just young and liked to goof off a little. Melissa liked to have fun, too, and had the most contagious, jovial (and sometimes really loud) laugh. But she would let me know with her adorable little "Stop it!" smirk that I was getting too goofy and needed to rein myself in. I actually loved it when she flashed me that smirk.

We had been spending time together for about a month, and I was quickly falling in love with her. One time when we were together, I started thinking, *I have to tell her. I have to tell her.*

The next time we were together was at her parents' house. We sat down in her living room, and I felt like we were in our own little world. We started talking, and my heart started beating really fast. I felt myself getting emotional. I was thinking, *This girl is unbelievable! I could marry this girl!* My heart kept racing, and I noticed my palms getting sweaty.

Tell her! Tell her! Tell! Her!

"Melissa, I just want you to know that I love you."

A shocked look came across her face, immediately followed by an expression that said, "I'm shocked, but I don't want to appear shocked." I wished I could unsay that one line.

An awkward silence lingered until Melissa let out a small sigh. "Jeremy, I appreciate that, but I can't tell you that right now. For me to say those words would be a pretty huge commitment."

I was both embarrassed and devastated. I was afraid I had freaked her out to the point that I had ruined whatever relationship could potentially develop between us.

I didn't sleep well that night. I kept replaying the scene in my head. But, I reasoned, I had needed to tell her. It was how I felt, and

I couldn't help it. She loved Jesus and she loved other people. There wasn't a hint of standoffishness or "too good" in her. If she saw someone who wasn't dressed in nice clothes or appeared to be down and out, she would go to that person and say, "How are you doing today? Jesus loves you!" She was amazing. She was the one for me. I was convinced of it. Yet had I become so caught up in my emotions that I had jumped the gun and ruined everything?

I had to keep asking that question for a couple of weeks because my declaration of love created a period of awkwardness between us. We weren't hanging out together every day, so I had a lot of time to analyze and speculate. During the times when we were together, I felt a need to convince her that I was normal. Then I thought how that approach could get weird because in trying to do things to prove I was normal, I could start doing things that weren't normal for me. I was in that confusing position where I started overthinking what I should do instead of just being myself.

Since we hadn't been seeing each other every day, I couldn't try to see her more often because that could look like I was trying too hard. But then I also couldn't see her less—to "give her room"—because that could look like I was trying to take a step back from her because she didn't say she loved me. Unfortunately I didn't know of a book titled *What to Do When You Say "I Love You" Too Soon* that I could read for advice. I was on my own to fix the mess I had created.

One thing I knew for sure was that I was not going to tell her "I love you" again until she said it to me next. I wasn't going to make that mistake a second time.

Crushed

Although the awkwardness lasted a few weeks, it seemed more like a few months. But we worked our way back to where we had been before my bomb in her parents' living room, and our relationship even began to grow beyond that point.

After we had recovered from my blunder, we recognized the time had come that I needed to let Jason know what was going on. I didn't know when or where or how I would tell him. I wasn't practicing a "So, Jason, we need to talk" speech, but I knew that when the first opportunity presented itself, I needed to start the conversation.

That opportunity came when a bunch of us were hanging out at the beach. Jason and I were off walking alone and he said, "Hey, I talked to Melissa last night." Jason called all the members of his Bible study periodically just to check in and see how they were doing. I felt bad for him, as he said he had called Melissa, because the lilt in his voice made it obvious he still had feelings for her.

"I gotta tell you something, man," I began. I paused so he would know that the "something" was serious. Little did I know that Melissa and her sister Heather were nervously watching from a distance, holding hands, and praying for our conversation.

"Melissa and I have been hanging out, and we both like each other."

"What?!" He asked if I was serious. When I said I was, he understandably became a little mad.

I kind of freaked out because I realized the conversation wasn't going to end well. It's not like I had expected Jason to say, "Oh, that's okay. It bums me out, but I'm okay." Certainly not. But he took the news hard—really hard. Telling him was much harder than I had expected.

"Out of all the girls, why Melissa?" he asked. "You know how I felt."

"It just happened," I said. I tried to explain myself but did a poor job. Truthfully, though, I'm not sure I could have given an explanation that would have made our discussion go better.

Jason was crushed and rightfully so, and nothing I could say was going to help.

He was upset, and I was feeling the impact of how badly I had hurt him. I dropped to my knees in the sand and cried.

"Dude, I'm so sorry," I said. "I don't want to do anything to hurt you."

But I had.

Jason was the type of guy everyone loved—*I* loved Jason. He had a loyal following, especially from his Bible study group, because he was a good leader who genuinely cared for the people he led. The phone calls he made to the group's members demonstrated that.

To the friends Jason and I shared, I looked like a jerk who had stolen Melissa from him. I didn't believe I had stolen her at all, but I became a bit of an outcast within that group. It took time for the wounds in those relationships to heal, but they eventually did. I still love Jason, and we still are good friends.

There was one person's negative reaction, however, that I was completely unprepared for: Melissa's.

When Melissa saw how badly Jason was hurt and how many of our friends defended him, friction developed between the two of us. If what we had done was wrong to that many people, Melissa wondered if our being together actually was wrong. I tried to convince her otherwise, that the others weren't supportive of our having a relationship only because they thought Jason had been wronged. They didn't know how sensitive we had tried to be toward Jason, how we had kept things quiet at first to gauge what there actually was between us before I talked to him.

"I care for you and you care for me," I would tell her. "We totally care for each other. We both love the Lord. There's nothing wrong with this."

"I just don't know," she would respond. "It seems like there's too much confusion around all this for it to be right."

We continued to date, but the fallout from my conversation with Jason dented our relationship. Jason and I remained friends, and

Melissa and Jason remained friends, but there was a noticeable distance that had entered into the relationships.

About a month after I told Jason about Melissa and me, the three of us were part of a group from Vista's college class that went on a missions trip to Maui. That was a great time of evangelizing in some of the island's poorer parts away from the tourist areas. We saw God do remarkable things in people's lives there.

But what had happened among Melissa, Jason, and me was a distraction. I think with the God-things that were taking place on our missions trip, we were all hyperaware of God's purpose in our being there and the importance of being fully focused on the Lord and what He wanted from us on that trip.

During some downtime, when Melissa and I were apart from the others on the beach, she told me she needed to break up with me. Her reasons were the same ones I had been trying to counter.

"It just doesn't seem right," she said. "There are too many issues and too much friction. With everything that's going on, I just don't feel like the Lord can be in this. I just need to be in the Word right now."

At CCBC, we guys would joke about the "Bible college way" a girl could break up with her boyfriend: "It's not you—I just need to be with Jesus. He's my boyfriend right now."

That wasn't what Melissa told me, but it sure felt that way. I was devastated. I had told her only that one time, but I loved her. I believed with all my heart that she was meant to be my wife. So, I did what any other mature young man being dumped by the woman of his dreams would do: I cried like a baby and called my mother.

"What's wrong with you women?" I asked my mom. "This is crazy. I thought she was the one!"

I had been crushed, and my mom knew without me having to say it. She listened as I vented, then in her typical calm, precise way redirected my focus from my perspective to God's perspective.

"Your only choice," she reminded me, "is to be patient and trust Him."

Did I hang up from my call with my mom and go skipping out to the beach, high-fiving everyone along the way? Of course not. I still hurt. I was still confused. I was still *crushed*. None of that changed. But my mom's advice caused me to pull back a little from everything I was feeling and look at the larger picture of the reason for the trip.

When I look back now, I do see one good result that came out of Melissa breaking up with me during that trip: It broke me to the point that I put all my focus on God for the rest of our time in Maui. In my brokenness, I saw how God could use me in amazing ways.

After Melissa broke up with me, God was the sole purpose of my trip. I would share the gospel with anyone, and people were accepting Christ as their Savior right there on the spot! Radical things were taking place. I walked up to a group of fifteen kids and started a conversation. They opened up to me and made me feel welcomed in their group. We were having a great talk. I started sharing some of the things that God had done in my life, then about Adam and Eve and how sin was brought into the world, and how Christ came to cover all that sin.

"Man, I love Jesus," I told them. "He's changed my life, and He can change your life."

Every kid in the group wound up bowing his head and praying to accept Christ. I had my picture taken with that group, and I still have that photo. Seeing my picture with those fifteen kids reminds me not of what I did but of what the Holy Spirit did. At a moment when I was completely emptied of myself, broken, and humbled, the Lord used me.

In fact, He probably was able to use me at that moment *because* I was completely emptied of myself, broken, and humbled.

Chapter 8

"JUST ONE PERSON"

Melissa and I still had the same group of friends, so after she broke up with me on the missions trip to Maui, we still saw each other every couple of weeks or so. Those meetings made me feel rather uneasy.

We "kind of, sort of" got back together for a brief period, but then she broke it off again.

Every time I saw Melissa, I hurt.

If we were in the same room, I would say something short to her, like "Hey," but for the most part I tried to avoid her. She still tried to be my friend and would want to start a conversation, but I couldn't handle seeing her and being just friends.

Near the end of summer 1999, I moved out of Grandma Marge's house after spending about a year and a half with her. Marge was a special woman, and the room and board she gave me truly was a gift from God. I can reflect now and see how God placed her in my life for more reasons than to give me a place to stay.

We had great discussions, and I learned from her years of experience serving the Lord. As I came to learn some of the events she had been through in her life, including the death of her husband, I was amazed at how she never questioned God. She knew the Lord was with her, she loved the Lord, and she seemed to anticipate that she was going to be with Him soon. I remember Grandma Marge as a faithful woman with a resolve that was both rock solid and sweet.

A friend from Vista, Danny, had asked if I wanted to share a place with him. By that point I was making enough from singing in churches that I could afford to pay my part of a bargain-rate rent, although I did have to eat more than my share of tuna, eggs, and ramen noodles to save money. (I ate so many ramen noodles that I won't even touch a package of them now.)

I was bumping into Melissa less frequently, but I still thought of her often and really missed being with her. In October, a friend told me Melissa had been having stomach pains and would have tests done to see what was causing them.

The day of her tests I went with a group of friends to visit her at her family's house. The test revealed she had a large but noncancerous cyst, and Melissa was her usual upbeat self.

It felt strange visiting Melissa in her family's home, but it was good to see her again. She was happy to see me, but, of course, she was the one who still wanted to be just friends. The group of us had decided to visit Melissa to let her know we cared about her, but I still really cared about her as more than just a friend, and I didn't want to linger at the house too long.

About that same time another door opened for me musically. With Jean-Luc as producer, I recorded my first CD: a ten-song, independently released project titled *Jeremy Camp: Burden Me*. We recorded it in San Diego at Horizon Christian Fellowship, thanks to pastor Mike MacIntosh.

I'm still grateful for Jean-Luc's mentoring and support after Melissa and I broke up. I was getting more opportunities to play in churches, and I continued to play sometimes with The Kry. Music helped me gradually move away from Melissa and on with my life.

I eventually reached the stage where I could accept that Melissa and I most likely were not going to get back together. I didn't even really want us to get back together because she had broken up with me (twice—kind of, sort of), and I didn't want to run the risk of getting hurt again.

Then in the spring of 2000, a friend asked if I had heard about Melissa.

"That cyst came back," he said, "and they took it out. And it is cancerous."

Cancerous? Melissa?

I wanted to go see her in the hospital—just as a friend—to support her.

It was a ninety-minute trip, and I became sentimental on the drive. My heart felt heavy for her. We had become distant friends and hadn't had much contact with each other, but we had shared a special time, and all those emotions came rushing back at me.

I did plenty of soul-searching during that drive, yet another time when I needed to die to myself and to be a friend. I couldn't be mad at her or hold it against her for breaking up with me. She needed friends, I told myself, and even though I had resolved to move on, I couldn't deny that I truly did still care about her.

Surprise in the Hospital

I felt strange walking up to the hospital front desk and asking for Melissa's room number. As I rode the elevator up to her floor, anxiety began building up within me.

I stepped off the elevator and walked to the waiting room, where some of Melissa's family and friends were sitting. There, I was told that Melissa had been diagnosed with ovarian cancer. She had undergone surgery to remove the cancer, but it was an aggressive form, and she would be starting chemotherapy immediately.

To hear that her cancer was aggressive and the urgency of starting chemo rattled me. Melissa's sister Heather told me she would go let Melissa know that I was there to see her. I didn't want to just burst into her room and say, "Hey! I'm here!"

I walked slowly down the hall to allow time for her to tell Melissa. As I neared Melissa's room, her parents, Mark and Janette, walked out. They were somber but seemed at peace.

Why are they leaving her room? I wondered. I didn't know how to act. I wanted to be there as a friend, but was I going to be viewed as the ex-boyfriend coming back?

"Hi," her parents said, smiling and embracing me. "Thanks for coming."

Mark and Janette walked away from the room, and my anxiety ratcheted up a notch. I didn't want to be in the room alone with Melissa. I didn't know what to expect. *Cancer* is an unnerving word, and I expected her to look sick and bummed out after having surgery.

I collected myself, took a deep breath, opened the door, and was shocked. Melissa was smiling from ear to ear with a supernatural glow. Her big ol' brown eyes were as bright as always.

Why is she so happy? She just found out she has cancer. I would be devastated.

"How are you doing?" I asked.

Her answer still inspires me: "If I were to die from this cancer and just one person accepted Jesus because of it, it would all be worth it."

Wow! What an answer!

I immediately felt both conviction and peace. Conviction because of my lack of faith compared to Melissa's, and peace just from being in her presence and seeing her eternal perspective while facing cancer. Melissa was willing to suffer if it meant *even only one person* would gain eternity in heaven! I've heard of others expressing something similar, and it's a sentiment many of us would hope to be able to live out, but those words took on a completely different context hearing a friend stricken with cancer say them as she lay in a hospital bed.

A verse came to mind: "For to me, to live is Christ and to die is gain."[5] As I later contemplated about receiving that verse in that moment, I realized that Paul was talking about not just our gain when we go to heaven but also the gain of others here on earth who would come to Jesus as they observed how we dealt with difficult circumstances.

Taped to the side of Melissa's bed, in her handwriting, were the words to the ballad "If You Want Me To" by Christian singer-songwriter Ginny Owens. The final verse is powerful:

> So take me on the pathway that leads me home to You
> And I will walk through the valley if You want me to.

I later had the privilege of getting to know Ginny and telling her how much her song meant to the two of us. The lyrics—especially the line "Gonna look into Your eyes and see You never let me down"—carry even more meaning considering Ginny has been blind since a very young age.

I can't remember what Melissa and I talked about or for how long we visited in her hospital room that day. But I do recall that, as I was leaving, I told her I would keep checking on how she was doing and come to see her when I could. I wanted to be a good friend for her.

Love Notes

The drive home from the hospital also was an emotional one. Melissa's first words to me about "just one person" and the way she was handling the situation were a reminder of the heart she had for Jesus and others, and how that was the reason I had fallen in love with her in the first place. The feelings I had for Melissa that I had apparently been suppressing rose up within me again. In trying to move on from our relationship, I had convinced myself that Melissa was wishy-washy. But I knew better. Melissa was an astounding young woman.

My mind began to play back memories of our time together—memories I had pushed away because recalling them hurt too much. As I allowed myself for the first time in a long while to reexperience my old feelings for Melissa, I became overwhelmingly sad over the staggering unknown of what was ahead for her because of the cancer.

As I drove, Ginny Owens's song "If You Want Me To" began playing on the radio. My eyes were so filled with tears that I thought I might have to pull my car over.

"Lord, what's going on?" I asked. And then I blurted out these words: "Lord, if she tells me that she loves me, I'll marry her!"

I didn't know why I said that, but I was certain those words had come from my heart. I spent that night praying for Melissa, crying, and longing to be near her again.

I called my parents the next day and told them about our visit and how my feelings for Melissa had been rekindled. My dad didn't say anything, so I asked what he was thinking.

"Well, son," he said, "you know if you go down this path, you might end up being with someone you have to take care of for the rest of your life. It won't be easy. Are you prepared to do that?"

In the emotion of the night before, I hadn't considered that. But none of that mattered. "Yes," I told my dad, "that would be okay."

I returned to visit Melissa in May, during her first round of chemotherapy. I expected she would be in pain or at the least very uncomfortable from the chemo. On my way to her family's home, I thought, *She's gonna tell me she loves me. I just know she's gonna say it.*

Melissa was in her bedroom when I arrived. She hadn't been feeling well, so she was lying in her bed.

I walked into her room with a big smile, wanting to be all cheerful for her. "Hey, how you doing?" I could tell from the weakened voice in her return greeting that the chemo had been tough.

We made small talk for a few minutes before her face indicated she had something serious to say.

"Jeremy," she began, "I never knew why it wasn't working between us. I know how you felt. And I always cared about you so much. But there was this reservation, and I didn't know why. Now I know why. It was God preparing me. He wanted me to be alone with Him for this time coming because of what I was about to face."

I nodded.

"I want to show you something," she said.

She pulled out her journals and began flipping to pages where she had written during our time apart from each other. The journals detailed how she had been praying for me and my future wife. "I cared about you so much," she continued. "I even met this guy in between us, but when we were hanging out, I couldn't stop thinking about you, and about how he wasn't you. When I saw you that day at the hospital, after all these months of praying, I knew I loved you."

I love you.

She said it! I couldn't believe it. I had hoped to hear her say that, and I had certainly dreamed of hearing those words. I had even had the feeling that she would say she loved me, but when she did, I responded in a way I didn't expect.

"This is—scary," I told her. "I don't know if I can do this. Please just give me some time."

Chapter 9

WALKING
BY FAITH

Melissa's "I love you" came just as I was preparing for a trip to Colorado to play a few concerts. She graciously told me to take as much time as I needed to think about our relationship. Melissa said she didn't expect me to make any type of commitment to her, but that she had needed to tell me she loved me so I would know how she felt. I told her I would come back to see her when I returned from Colorado.

I know what some readers may be thinking at this point: *Are you serious?! She just opened up and said she loved you, and you promised God that you would marry her if she did. How can you back out now?*

I wasn't trying to back out on the promise I had made to God about marrying her. Marriage is a big commitment as it is, and I realized—as my dad had advised me—that because of the cancer, a marriage with Melissa likely would face enormous pressures right off the bat. I was the one with the let's-do-this personality, but there were so many X factors that I needed time to process what might lie ahead for us.

One of the concert hosts in Colorado put me up in a quiet cabin in the mountains. It was a perfect place to pray and reflect. The day I was there, I stayed up most of the night praying and asking God what He wanted me to do about Melissa. It was such a long, emotional, and sleepless night that the next day as I prepared for that night's concert, I thought I had an idea of what Jacob might have felt like following his night of wrestling with God.

As I sought God, I remembered the words of James 1:5: "If any of you lacks wisdom, you should ask God, who gives generously to all without finding fault, and it will be given to you."

Boy, was I ever asking God for His wisdom. On my own I could not answer the question of what I should do next. I knew what I had said I would do, but I did not know how marrying Melissa would fit in with what God had called me to do in music. God's answer to me: *You've asked Me, son. She has responded to what you asked Me in the way that you hoped she would. What more do you need?*

The words came clear to me, but still I struggled with fear. I tried to follow the instruction of Matthew 6:34: "Therefore do not worry about tomorrow, for tomorrow will worry about itself. Each day has enough trouble of its own." I tried, but it wasn't easy. On the trip, I connected with John David Webster, a musician friend who lived in the Rockies. He could tell something was on my mind and suggested we take a drive into the mountains. He took me to a spot where we could sit on a large rock and look out over the beautiful mountains. It was an amazing place to be reminded of God's power and majesty.

I told John David about my relationship with Melissa, about what I had said I would do if she said "I love you," and the uncertainty surrounding Melissa's health.

"If you love her with all your heart," John David said, "you can't let fear have any place in the matter. You just have to do what God has called you to do. You can't consider the future. Go where the Lord has led you, then trust Him for the rest."

Trust Him for the rest.

Those words echoed in my mind as though they were bouncing around the Colorado mountains. I looked out at the breathtaking scenery and considered just how big God must be. He had created everything I could see from my seat on that rock, and so much more. If He could be in control and hold steady the entire earth, there could be no doubt that He could hold little me steady. It's like the old children's song says, God has the whole world in His hands. And that included me.

There was only one thing I could say to God after considering that: "I will trust You!"

As I had told Melissa I would, I went to see her at her parents' house as soon as I returned from Colorado. She said it had been a rough day, and she wasn't feeling well. Her long brown hair had started to thin out because of the treatments. But, typical Melissa, instead of focusing on her situation, she wanted to know how I was doing and how the concerts in Colorado had gone. After we had chatted for a while in the living room, she said she wanted to go outside onto the front lawn and get some fresh night air.

I was concerned about her because even though she didn't want to let on that anything was bothering her, she seemed pretty bummed out.

"Are you okay?" I asked.

"I'm okay," she said.

"What's going on? I can tell something's wrong."

"I'm okay," she said again.

I looked directly into her eyes. "Look, Melissa, if we're going to get married, you're going to have to be able to tell me everything you're going through."

"Married? Are you asking me to marry you?"

I could see tears in her eyes and feel the ones in mine.

"I love you," I said. "And I see God's hand and His plan in this whole thing, in how He orchestrated it. I see that He brought us together."

We were still crying, but we both started laughing.

It was a spontaneous moment, for sure. I hadn't bought a ring, and I hadn't asked her parents' blessing before proposing.

We walked back into the house where her parents were. "Hey, can we talk to you guys?" Melissa said. "We're going to get married!"

Her parents were super stoked. I got along really well with them, and they knew how much I cared for Melissa, how much she cared for me, and how much we both loved the Lord. What they wanted most was for their daughter to be happy, and I still can visualize the look of pure happiness on Melissa's face that night.

On my ramen noodles, tuna, and eggs income, I couldn't afford an engagement ring. Melissa's mother gave her a ring that had belonged to Melissa's grandmother.

Even though it had been a rough day, Melissa had gone for a run/walk but hadn't taken her postworkout shower when I arrived at her house. She joked many times later how she had always imagined that her proposal would be a glamorous scene, but instead she had felt all "sweaty and gross" when I proposed. Of course, she looked great to me, and Melissa would add to her joking that the proposal actually turned out better than any way she had dreamed it would happen.

I hadn't told my parents that I planned to propose, but I had told them about Melissa saying she loved me and that I had promised God I would marry her if she said that. I couldn't wait to tell them that we were engaged. But I had to. Because of the time difference between California and Indiana, I didn't call my parents until the next morning. My mom was home when I called.

"I asked her!" I excitedly reported.

Concerning Call

Melissa and I set October 21 as our wedding date. It was only five months away, but we didn't want a long engagement. Both of us had 100 percent certainty about marrying the other, so there didn't seem to be a reason to wait. We wanted to be together. I hated having to say "See you tomorrow" at the end of the night. I wanted to spend all my time with Melissa.

I also wanted to help her deal with the effects of her chemotherapy treatments as much as I could. Because we weren't married, there were obvious limitations on how much I could help Melissa, but her family was very sweet about allowing me to be a part of her care. There were nights when I would be at their house late and get sleepy, and her parents would offer to let me spend the night on their living room couch.

As would be expected for someone going through chemo, Melissa had difficult days. Anyone who has been through chemo, or been close to someone who has, knows what a physical and mental battle the treatments are. In the big picture medically, though, things seemed to be going well, but with cancer there is always a cloud of uneasiness that hangs over you.

Melissa and I knew the importance of staying in God's Word and receiving hope and strength from it at that time, both on our own and together. A key verse for me then was Jeremiah 29:13: "You will seek me and find me when you seek me with all your heart." We were seeking God with all our hearts and finding Him. We attended church together, and even on the days when she was weakened by the chemo, she continued to worship with her same unrestrained passion.

That was a period I can look back on and identify that my faith was growing. One reason it grew was because of Melissa. Even though my faith had increased greatly, being around Melissa made me feel convicted about my need for an even deeper faith. I was serious about my Bible study and my walk with the Lord, but hey, I was young. I could have those silly moments with friends during Bible study or get a little lax in my devotion time periodically. But Melissa—man, she had an all-out devotion to God. She was constantly reading the Bible and praying. She never seemed to miss an opportunity to talk with someone about Jesus. She was so focused on her relationship with the Lord and being a shining example for Him.

Sometimes when we were together, she would walk away from me to go talk with someone else. I'd be like, "Hey, I'm here too." But then I'd watch her talk to that person and share Jesus with him or her, and it would hit me how many opportunities were around us that she would see and I would miss. When their conversation would end, and I would see how that person responded to Melissa, I'd say to myself, "That was so unbelievable."

I think *our* faith was growing too. As a couple, we both benefited from an assurance that we were supposed to be together, and in a sense that assurance overshadowed the uncertainty of the cancer. We still were concerned about Melissa's health and praying consistently and expectantly for healing, but we shared a joy from knowing that God had brought us into each other's paths and had created one path for us to walk together. The joy of the Lord indeed was our strength.[6] That joy was possible because joy does not come from circumstances that can change with the result of a test or a sudden pain. Joy comes from having a relationship with the unchanging God and transcends any trial we can face on earth. Even though Melissa battled weakness, pain, and nausea from her treatments, we laughed a lot together. We learned to be thankful and content in all circumstances.[7] When her hair had completely fallen out, I began calling her "my beautiful, bald-haired, brown-eyed babe." That would draw a good laugh from her. And I meant it every time. With or without hair, she was beautiful to me because as attractive as Melissa was on the outside, she had an even more incredible inner beauty. In fact, as we made wedding plans and looked ahead to our life together, Melissa became more beautiful to me.

We talked about going into ministry together. I would sing, and with the love Melissa had for people, she would minister to women and lead Bible studies. It seemed like a perfect fit to us.

Melissa had been studying to become a teacher, and I knew she would be a great one because I had observed how she interacted with kids and youth at church, hugging them and giving them her big smile that made each one feel as though her smile was exclusively for them. And I couldn't wait to watch her with our kids. We talked about having children and all the dreams engaged couples have of chasing little ones around the house and taking them to sports activities or to recitals or whatever their interests would be.

Late in the summer of 2000, we flew to Indiana to attend the wedding of Joey Bell, a friend I'd known since I was young and with whom I had attended Bible college. Melissa knew my parents from their trips to California to visit me, but that was the first time she visited my home. It was cool to share parts of my past with her, and, being Melissa, she instantly hit it off with the friends I introduced her to.

I had one friend whose mother had cancer and, like Melissa, was going through chemo treatments. Melissa went over to their house to help cook soup for his mother. She understood what my friend's mother was going through and wanted to serve her and do what she could to help.

While we were in Indiana, Melissa received a phone call from one of her doctors. A test result showed there was cancer on her uterus and the doctor wanted Melissa to undergo a hysterectomy as soon as possible. That news jarred us. If Melissa had her uterus removed, we wouldn't be able to have kids.

When we returned home and met with the doctor, I told him that we were going to have people all around the country and the world praying for us.

"If you go in for the operation and there's no cancer on her uterus," I asked, "you won't remove it, right?"

"Of course we wouldn't," he answered. But then he looked directly at me and, in a no-nonsense manner to make sure I understood the seriousness of the situation, added, "But we've done the tests, and it's there. I'm sorry."

Mr. and Mrs. Camp!

The operation was scheduled for as soon as possible, and we sent out a call to everyone we knew—and asked them to ask everyone *they* knew—to intercede on Melissa's behalf. The praying continued through the operation.

I paced the hallways of the hospital. *God, You are the healer*, I would pray. *We need Your healing power today. Please heal Melissa.*

After a shorter time than we had expected to wait, Melissa's mom came running toward me. "It's gone!" she exclaimed. "The cancer is gone! They didn't remove her uterus!"

I dropped to my knees right there in the hallway. "Thank You, God! Thank You!" I called my family and as many friends as I could think of, excitedly sharing the news: "God healed her! He did it!"

The surgeon said he had found no trace of the cancer on her uterus. When Melissa woke up from her surgery and learned the great news, we cried together at the realization that we could still have kids together.

Her whole attitude toward being healed was as though she knew all along that would be the outcome. For me, I had wanted her to be healed and had believed that she could be healed, but I hadn't necessarily known it would happen. Melissa had known. Once again, I was amazed and inspired by her faith.

Melissa turned twenty-one on October 7. Fourteen days later, we were married in Rancho Santa Fe, with my dad performing the ceremony.

Melissa was excited that her hair had begun to grow back out for the wedding. It was a little spiky, and we made a few jokes about that just as we had when she was my beautiful, bald-haired, brown-eyed babe.

She was stunningly gorgeous in her wedding dress. As she walked down the aisle toward me, her face was a glowing reflection of Christ's peace and joy. Melissa had chosen white as the color for all the bridesmaids' dresses to represent the purity that we stood for.

The bride and the groom are the natural center of attention at a wedding, but we wanted our ceremony to be one in which God was honored and glorified. The sweet presence of the Holy Spirit filled the sanctuary throughout our ceremony. Together we sang Hillsong's "Dwelling Places," which we chose to express how our love for each other was rooted in God. The chorus lines say, "I love You, I love You, I love You, and my heart will follow wholly after You."

Melissa's bout with cancer added to the emotion everyone in the church obviously felt during the ceremony. Melissa had wanted to invite everyone she had ever known—there were about six hundred in attendance—because she wanted them to hear the gospel proclaimed during the service.

We hadn't been able to afford on our own the type of wedding that Melissa probably had dreamed of, but because she was so loved, friends rallied around us and helped provide what I think Melissa considered a picture-perfect wedding. The ceremony was a joyous time, and Melissa obviously loved every minute of it.

We were happy to have Jason Duff attend. Time had healed the wound in my relationship with him, and I appreciated the gracious support he showed Melissa and me by being there.

Melissa and I flew off for a two-week honeymoon in Hawaii, where her aunt and uncle owned a house on the beach. We had the house to ourselves for a week, and when her aunt and uncle came over for the second week, we stayed in a downstairs apartment-type area. Her aunt and uncle were another blessing for us because we would not have been able to afford two weeks in Hawaii on our own. We also were going to see my family in Indiana for a couple of weeks, so we would have about a month after the wedding before returning home to California.

From the moment our plane landed on Oahu, the trip truly did feel like a getaway. Melissa had been feeling progressively stronger as the wedding approached, and our honeymoon was a time for us to be alone together and not have to deal with chemo treatments or doctors' appointments.

We started off our honeymoon just enjoying being married and having all our plans ahead of us. We walked along the beach and swam in the ocean. We rode bicycles to sightsee along the coast. We went out for dinners. We stayed in and made meals together. We played board games and Phase 10. We did whatever we wanted to do—basically, we hung out. We simply had fun while it soaked in that we were married!

The whole scene—being married to Melissa, being able to honeymoon in Hawaii despite not having enough money to do so—seemed like a dream.

Although being in Hawaii was a time of relief from the health issues Melissa had dealt with back home, I still felt a seriousness inside as though I did not know how to fully let go. There were moments when the reality of her situation hit me.

One of those moments came when I was alone in the living room. I was reflecting on 2 Corinthians 5:7, "For we walk by faith, not by sight" (NASB), and I sensed God speaking into my heart: *I know you're afraid and there is a lot you don't know. But you're just not supposed to know right now. Just continue to trust Me. I know what I'm doing. I know what I'm doing.*

God was right—I did not know what was going to happen. I didn't even have a clue what might happen. Although things were looking better with Melissa's health and we were daring to say her cancer was in remission, I was scared. But I thought of God's words to continue to trust Him and recalled some of the reasons from my past that served as evidence for why I could continue to trust. With one breath God had puffed life into me, and He had been faithful to me for all my life.

I grabbed my guitar and pondered two questions: Will I believe God when He says His hand will guide my every way? Will I receive the words He says, every moment of every day?

The words to the song "Walk by Faith" came to me:

(Verse 1)
Would I believe You when You would say
Your hand will guide my every way?
Will I receive the words You say
Every moment of every day?

[Chorus]
Well I will walk by faith even when I cannot see
Well because this broken road prepares Your will for me

(Verse 2)
Help me to rid my endless fears
You've been so faithful for all my years
With one breath You make me new
Your grace covers all I do.

Yeah, yeah, yeah, yeah, yeah, yeah

[Chorus]

[Bridge]
Well I'm broken, but I still see Your face
Well You've spoken, pouring Your words of grace

[Chorus, twice]

Well hallelujah, hallelu
(I will walk by faith)
Well hallelujah, hallelu
(I will walk by faith)

I will walk, I will walk, I will walk by faith
I will, I will, I will walk by faith[8]

I had been reading what God's Word said. I had been listening to what He had spoken to me. Melissa and I had been trusting Him. But now I was at a point where there was one major question I needed to confront: Am I going to take action on my faith? The chorus answered that question with resolve: I would follow the Lord wherever He led me, regardless of what might lie ahead.

I played and sang the song for Melissa. "It's beautiful," she said, and we sat there quietly, I think both feeling the same peace that God was leading us and would continue to do so no matter what we would face together.

A few days later Melissa said she was having stomach pain. "It feels weird," she said, "like it's swelling." Her eyes revealed a deep concern.

"Maybe it's just something you've eaten," I told her. We had been eating different foods on the trip from what we typically ate. I took a seat in the living room and began to feel nervous. I hoped Melissa had indigestion. But once someone has had cancer, you can hope a pain is from something minor, but there is always the fear it's much worse.

We still had a great time on the rest of our honeymoon. But on a complete getaway from our daily routines, we had a lot of time to think. There were moments I had to myself when my thoughts would return to what Melissa had said about her stomach. I would get concerned, and some nights I had trouble sleeping.

I tried not to look worried, but I think Melissa sensed moments of anxiety and fear in me. I could tell she also was wondering what was going on inside her body. But any concerns she expressed were about me, not her.

"Are you okay?" she would ask me.

"I'm fine," I would say, blown away on the inside that she was thinking more about me than herself.

Chapter 10

SEEKING HOPE

Melissa and I flew from Hawaii to Indiana. We were having a reception there for those who had not been able to travel to California for our wedding, and a friend who was a part of our wedding was also getting married.

The weather was relatively warm for an Indiana autumn. My parents were having a new driveway poured at their house, and everyone in the family stepped barefoot into the wet cement. I don't know what says "Welcome to the family" to a newlywed more than letting her put her footprints in her in-laws' driveway! Beneath all the footprints, we wrote "Isaiah 52:7," which says, "How beautiful on the mountains are the feet of those who bring good news, who proclaim peace, who bring good tidings, who proclaim salvation, who say to Zion, 'Your God reigns!'"

My mom was helping set up and decorate for my friend's wedding, and Melissa wanted to help. But she wasn't feeling well, and my mom was trying to make sure she didn't get overtaxed. My mom told Melissa that she needed to rest because she was probably worn out from the treatments, and then everything having to do with the wedding, and then the drastic time changes in traveling to Hawaii and then back to the Midwest.

But my parents were concerned, and I told them I would make an appointment with Melissa's doctor as soon as we were back in California. I also told them how excited I was to be going back home. Melissa had already fixed up our apartment, and a month after marrying, we were finally going to settle into our home.

When we returned home, I made an appointment for Melissa. This was right around Thanksgiving, and Heather had come home to visit her family. Heather later told me that she and Melissa were alone in the bedroom and that she could tell Melissa wasn't feeling well.

"What's wrong?" Heather asked.

Melissa partly lifted her shirt, took Heather's hand, and rubbed it across her stomach. Heather could feel tumors all over her stomach, and they began to weep together and pray that God would heal whatever was wrong with Melissa.

When the doctor examined Melissa, he said she had fluid buildup in her stomach that needed to be drained. As the fluid was drained, I held tightly to her hand and felt helpless as the pained expressions kept appearing on her face. That was difficult to watch. The doctor had the fluids tested, and when the results came back, he came into Melissa's room and asked to speak alone with me in the hallway.

Oh no, I thought as I stood from my chair and made my way toward the door.

"What's going on?" I asked the doctor outside the room before he had a chance to start the conversation. I saw compassion in his eyes. He knew we had just married.

"I'm afraid the cancer is—well, it's all over her," he told me. "It has returned, and it has metastasized to other parts of her body. I'm sorry to have to tell you this."

The news hit me like a punch, but it was more of a get-your-attention jab than a knockout blow. I still had my let's-get-after-it mentality from writing "Walk by Faith." We'd received bad news before and Melissa had been healed, and I was ready to put together an action plan to deal with this next problem too.

"Okay, so what do we do now?" I asked the doctor.

He didn't answer immediately, and I didn't like how intently he looked into my eyes.

"No, see," he said slowly, "there's nothing else we can do."

"What do you mean?" I asked.

"Our treatment options are very few. Jeremy, she probably has months or maybe even weeks to live."

I don't remember how the conversation ended. Where my memory picks up again, I was alone in the hallway, realizing I needed to compose myself as quickly as I could. Then I walked into the room to tell Melissa.

Because the doctor had taken me out of the room, she had to have known that the news wasn't good. I could tell she had been crying, and she likely could see from my eyes that I had been crying too.

I sat beside her bed and repeated what the doctor had told me. We both broke down crying. She started trying to console me, but we didn't say much while we waited for her to be released to go home.

I was in disbelief as I drove home and don't remember anything we talked about until one thing she said that I can still hear crystal clear in her voice to this day: "I want to let you know that it's okay if you find somebody else after I go, and I don't want you to have to wait. You don't have to sit in this grief for a long time."

I couldn't understand why she told me that. "We're in a fight here," I told her. "I'm still gonna fight."

It wasn't that Melissa was choosing not to fight, but she already was coming to grips with the reality of her condition and looking ahead to help me with what *I* would be facing.

I called my parents to inform them of the doctor's report.

"Hello?" my mom answered.

I tried to speak, but I couldn't. I tried again and still couldn't.

My mom hung up the phone. I waited a few seconds to gather myself and dialed the number again, but no one answered.

I called my sister.

"Hello?" she answered.

Again I tried to speak, but couldn't. April hung up. I called back. She answered. I failed again to say anything. She hung up again. I called a third time.

"Please don't hang up," I barely managed to say when she answered. April stayed on the line. I had difficulty talking.

"They just told me," I managed, "Melissa has a few weeks to a few months to live."

I told April how I had tried to call my mom and she had hung up, and how I had called back and she hadn't answered. My parents didn't have cell phones, but April said she knew my parents had an appointment with the banker and that she would track them down for me. April called the bank, and when the banker's secretary stepped into his office and told my mom that April was on the phone, her heart sank. She knew something was terribly wrong if April had called the bank. April told my mom what I had said, and my parents left immediately to return home and call me.

"We're coming out," my mom told me. "We'll do whatever we need to do to get there."

"No, don't come yet," I told her. "I want to see if I can find some different options for Melissa. We're going to look at some things we can do. I don't even know if we'll be here, so wait."

Fighting, Believing, and Worshipping

It became obvious right away that we would not be fighting alone. For the past several months, we had been reaching out to as many people as we could to pray for Melissa. We tapped into our prayer network again after receiving the bad news from the doctor.

Ministers and friends began coming to our apartment to pray for Melissa and anoint her with oil. During some of those visits, we had powerful times of worship and praise. We heard from friends and family who lived outside of our area and wanted to let us know they were praying and believing for healing.

Although we were disappointed with the diagnosis of her cancer returning, we were so confident that the Lord could heal her. I really struggled with seeing her in pain, so I wanted healing to come quickly.

"Please, God," I would plead, "heal Melissa."

My mom would call almost every day with a scripture that God had given her to share with us. The verses were filled with encouragement, exhortation, and comfort. They reminded us of God's goodness during difficult circumstances, and they pointed us to saints who served as examples of walking through the fire and coming out on the other side with a deeper faith.

We were blessed with financial gifts, with a big thanks to Joey Buran. Joey was a Hall of Fame surfer known as the "California Kid," who had become a pastor at Calvary Chapel Costa Mesa. He had recently founded a youth outreach named Worship Generation. I played at some of Joey's events, and we became good friends.

When Joey learned Melissa's cancer had returned and spread, he began telling people in his congregation and on a live radio broadcast of his Worship Generation service about Melissa. He suggested that people send us money and gave out our mailing address. Friends and even people we didn't know started sending us checks and notes of encouragement.

Because of those gifts, I was able to take some time off from scheduling concerts and church services so I could spend my time with Melissa. I had to take Melissa to the hospital about every three days to have her stomach drained. There was so much fluid building up that on some visits they drained up to seven liters.

I hated those drainings because it was a painful procedure for Melissa. When I would see the winces on her face and hear her soft moans, I would practically plead with God to heal her right there so the pain would stop. It was a helpless feeling to watch my wife ache and not be able to do anything about it. I knew my being beside Melissa was a big help for her, but I felt so inadequate when she hurt.

The pain would continue when we returned home. Melissa was tough and tried to keep the focus off her suffering, but I remember one evening when she was lying on the couch in the living room and groaning in pain.

"Can you pull out your guitar," she asked me, "and can we worship?"

It wasn't a question I was expecting, but I quickly grabbed my guitar and sat close to her. We sang a song called "Good to Me."

There is a part of the song where the words "for You are good" are repeated several times. I had been singing with my head down and eyes closed, and one of the times when I was singing "for You are good," I looked up and saw Melissa—weakened and hurting—singing along with both hands raised to the Lord. The next words couldn't get past my throat because I broke down at the sight of her unshakeable faith.

No matter how badly Melissa suffered, she continued to praise God. I would hear her tell God, "You are good. In the midst of the hardships and pain, You are good. Our circumstances don't make sense, but You are good." That reminded me of what I had heard my dad say many times while I was growing up: "Life is hard, but God is good."

We knew God could heal her instantaneously or through medicine and doctors blessed with God-given abilities to treat patients. In addition to all our prayers, we tried holistic treatments such as making changes in Melissa's diet, drinking carrot juice, and eating garlic soup and other foods believed to fight cancer.

We explored treatment options in Mexico. We visited a run-down facility in Tijuana that had limos to transport people who had run out of hope from treatment in the States. Inside, the nurses were dressed in all white and wore hats with red crosses. They gave Melissa medication we couldn't get back home, and then we drove back across the border to have Melissa's abdomen drained again at the hospital.

We also flew to Houston, Texas, to visit the MD Anderson Cancer Center.

I called my mom after we arrived in Houston. "This is so hard because she's so weak," I said. "We had to get a wheelchair for her because she was so weak."

We were optimistic for a positive report from one of the best hospitals in the nation for cancer treatment, and the MD Anderson doctors did give us some hope. They told us that Melissa's cancer was Stage III instead of Stage IV. They also said that while she had received the proper type of treatment in California, the treatment had been stopped too soon. They told us to have her doctors restart the treatment and that might make a difference. The doctors also told us there were smaller things that we could do that might help her, such as increase her protein intake.

But after we returned from Houston, Melissa began to rapidly lose weight.

Because she had been unable to keep her food down, Melissa had to spend Christmas in the hospital. Her sister Megan had to undergo an emergency operation on Christmas Day, and their family was able to get them beds in the same room. Melissa had been really sad about having to be in the hospital during Christmas, but when Megan became her roommate, her family put up some decorations in the room and created a festive atmosphere.

But after Melissa left the hospital, the amount of time between the awful drainings shrank. Her pain increased in intensity and frequency.

I was trying to be strong for Melissa, but it was difficult. Several times when I knew Melissa couldn't hear me, I called my parents.

One of my parents would answer, and I would just break down crying.

"It's so hard," I'd say.

I considered myself as fighting alongside Melissa. I wanted to be an encouragement for her. But there were times when I thought, *I can't do this anymore. This is just too much—it's too painful.*

But each time, God would send me a wave of strength that enabled me to continue fighting. And Melissa seemed to know what I needed, too, because she would suggest, "Let's worship the Lord." To be honest, many times when she said that, worshipping was about the last thing I wanted to do. But each time, because she wanted to, I would get my guitar and sing along with her, praising God for all His goodness. Over and over, God used our time of worship to resupply us with the strength only He could provide.

We kept placing our trust in God. We still talked about our future, even continuing to dream about one day having kids running around our home. A friend gave us an illustrated children's book as a gift of hope, and we clutched that book as a sign to dare to imagine better days ahead.

Chapter 11

"IT'S TIME"

I wasn't performing much music while Melissa was sick because I wanted to be with her as much as I could. We didn't want to waste one moment we could have together, so on the few occasions when I did take part in an event, Melissa went with me when able.

Horizon Christian Fellowship had asked me to be a part of their New Year's Eve outreach at the convention center in San Diego. Melissa was unable to walk well by that point, but she wanted to go with me in her wheelchair. It required a lot of strength for her just to be there.

The set that night included my first public performance of "Walk by Faith." I shared with the audience the story behind the song—about Melissa and how the song had come to me on our honeymoon, and then what had taken place following our honeymoon.

I began singing but, truthfully, wasn't really feeling the words as I sang them. I hope that doesn't come off as me being insincere about the song because that wasn't the case. That is a deep song that came at a moment when God was ministering to me, and I believe He gave me the words so that He could minister to others through my music. Over the past decade, I've heard from literally hundreds of people who wanted me to know how much that particular song has helped them.

That night, though, there was just so much going on inside my brain because of Melissa's deteriorating health.

Melissa was in her wheelchair to the side of the stage, and when I neared the end of the song and was singing the hallelujahs, I looked to my left at Melissa. She was very skinny. Her face had thinned. I knew how weak she had become. But there she was with hands held high, singing with every ounce of strength she had, "Hallelujah"—our translation of the Hebrew for "Praise ye the Lord."

She was having the same type of intimate moment with the Lord as when she first caught my eye at the Bible study at Palomar College. On the exterior, Melissa had changed dramatically since then. But despite everything that had happened to her, her faith in God had not weakened. Instead, it had strengthened.

When I saw Melissa praising God, I felt a Holy Spirit moment come across me like a strong wind. His power that I felt on that stage was incredible. It was another wave of strength that came exactly when I needed it.

All right, I thought, *let's keep going.*

It wasn't too long, though, until the arrival of the day I had dreaded, and had even tried to prevent myself from looking ahead to. Melissa needed around-the-clock care in a hospital.

Melissa's mother and sister Heather had helped care for her. We had also had some outside assistance. For a couple of weeks, Melissa had needed continuous care from us. She would dehydrate easily, so we had to change out her hydration pack. I would be awakened during the middle of the night by the beep of the equipment alerting me that it was time to change her stent to keep her hydrated. I also would wake up on my own during the night just to make sure she was okay, so I wasn't sleeping much or well.

Melissa's pain was probably the most difficult part for me. Her pain had worsened and grown more frequent. There was a painkiller I would give her, but if the pain reached the excruciating level before

I gave her the shot, it would be too late for the medicine to take effect. One time when she woke up in great pain I didn't get the medicine in fast enough. That was one of the worst nights of my life to see her in agony and feel like it was my fault, that I had failed her. She had hard days, and she had days when she would be understandably irritable because of the pain. But I never once heard Melissa complain about the pain or question God.

I stayed by her side all the time, but there were times when she would lovingly look at me and say, "I just need some alone time with the Lord." I wouldn't want to leave the apartment in case she needed to cry out to me for something, so I would go into the bathroom and pray.

God, seriously! You've got to do something—take her home or stop the pain or heal her. But this being-in-limbo thing . . .

But Melissa's pain wasn't going away. It was becoming more constant, and we could no longer give her the care she needed at home. Placing Melissa in a hospital felt like taking a step toward finality that we would never be able to take back. I hurt at the likelihood that if God didn't provide a miraculous healing, Melissa and I would never again be home together.

Melissa had been in the hospital only a few days when her condition noticeably worsened. One of the doctors said they would do everything they could "to keep her comfortable." I didn't like hearing that. It sounded like the doctor was giving up. Fatigued and frustrated, I took it out on the doctor, getting in his face and yelling, "No, we're not just waiting this out! Until the last day, we are going to pray for healing, trust the Lord, and not give up! We believe that God heals, and I'm not going to give up!"

Also, a doctor—I can't recall if it was the same doctor—gave Melissa a book. I overheard him tell her the book was on how to prepare for the final days. When the doctor came out of the room, I stopped him.

"Hey, don't be giving her that book and basically say she's gonna die," I told him, "because we're going to continue to have hope to the last day. *Don't* be doing that kind of stuff."

"Listen," the doctor calmly told me, "you need to face what's happening now. You need to face reality."

"Reality," I responded, "is that God can heal her."

I continued to believe that God could heal Melissa and continued to pray that He would. While Melissa slept, I'd sit beside her bed, watching her, watching the monitors hooked up to her for even the slightest change—in either direction—in her numbers. And I would pray over and over and over, *God, please heal her. Please heal my wife.*

I would lay a pillow on the tile floor in Melissa's room, put a blanket over me, and fall asleep. I didn't like leaving her side, but sometimes I would go down to the hospital chapel and sleep there because it had padded pews.

Our families were with us the entire time, along with a steady flow of friends into and out of the waiting room, bringing us flowers, cards of encouragement, and praying for us. As she had her entire life, Melissa remained concerned first and foremost about others. She greeted visitors by asking how they were doing. She would take hold of someone's hand, grip it as tightly as she could, smile at them, and make sure they understood how much she appreciated not just their visit but them.

Melissa always had a knack for knowing how and when to encourage others. One morning when my mom and dad were sitting with her, she told them, "I want you to know how much I love you both. You are the in-laws I prayed for, and the Lord brought you into my life."

She loved roses—yellow and red roses. There always seemed to be roses in her room that someone had brought to her. Visitors would receive a rose from Melissa, and she then would pray for them. She also would have members of her family deliver roses to other patients she had met. Her father was able to pray with other patients every day because of the rose deliveries.

Melissa still enjoyed singing. Friends would bring guitars into her room to play worship songs, and she would sing along. One day when she was especially tired, I looked at her and said, "We're going to beat this."

She started softly singing, "Jesus loves me, this I know." As we sang the rest of the song together, she raised her thinned arms, not as high as she normally would but as high as she could. A minute or two after finishing the song, she fell asleep.

The timeline while Melissa was in the hospital is still very fuzzy to me, but I think we were there for about two weeks. At one point, with her condition still worsening, she was moved into a critical-care area so she could receive a higher level of medical attention. Within a few days after that move, she began to slip in and out of consciousness. Her awake time became less and less, but the hospital staff was able to better manage her pain with increased levels of medication. Seeing Melissa suffer less with pain helped and made me regret even more than I already had my confronting the doctor who said they would keep Melissa comfortable.

Melissa prayed with every doctor before every shot she received or every procedure she underwent, and one of the nurses had been taking note of the faith of Melissa and those of us around her. The nurse saw the praying, heard the songs of praise, felt the peace in Melissa's room, and sensed something was missing in her own life.

Melissa had been praying for the nurse and asked those of us staying with her to pray for the nurse as well. Melissa's dad prayed with the nurse one day, and she asked Jesus to come into her heart and be her Lord and Savior.

If I were to die from this cancer and just one person accepted Jesus because of it, it would all be worth it.

Melissa didn't have much strength when told of the nurse's decision, but she cried at learning that her purpose in her suffering had been accomplished. I think that confirmation was a beautiful gift to Melissa from God, saying, *What you said, I have made come to fruition. I wanted you to see this happen.*

"Remember that 'one person'?" I said to Melissa. "This is just the beginning. There will be many more."

With Jesus

Melissa was sleeping one night when I sensed the Lord wanting me to take my guitar into an open waiting room next door and read from Psalms, a book that many times had been a source of comfort for me. David's psalms reveal the raw honesty with which he poured out his heart to God. There is a clear trend in David's psalms: he tells God of his trial and his hurt, asks why that trial is occurring, and then declares his trust in God and God's unfailing loving-kindness and mercy.

I began reading and felt God leading me to Psalm 119, where verses 153–154 say, "Consider my affliction and deliver me, for I do not forget Your law. Plead my cause and redeem me; revive me according to Your word" (NKJV).

"Revive me." That's what I needed—reviving. In that empty room I wrote the song "Revive Me."

(Verse 1)
Consider my affliction and please deliver me
Plead my cause and redeem me
Salvation is not for the wicked
For they don't seek Your word
Great are Your tender mercies, Lord.

[Chorus]
Revive me, according to Your loving-kindness
Revive me, that I may seek Your Word
Revive me, according to Your loving-kindness
Revive me, oh Lord.

(Verse 2)
You give me understanding according to Your Word
Great peace for those who seek Your face
I long for salvation
My lips shall praise Your name
I rejoice in the treasure of Your keep.

[Bridge]
For all my ways are before You
I let Your hand become my help
My soul longs and adores You
Let my cry come before You, oh Lord.[9]

After I had written the final words, I returned to Melissa's room. She was awake, and I asked if I could sing the song for her. Tears flowed from our eyes.

"It's beautiful," she said.

"God gave this to me for us right now," I told her.

In the ensuing hours, Melissa became less responsive. We could tell that her body was shutting down, that her time was nearing.

About ten of us were in Melissa's room, still crying and praying for healing. It had been several hours since she had responded to any of us. Mike MacIntosh, our pastor friend from Horizon church, walked over to me and whispered, "I think you need to let her know it's okay, that she can go be with the Lord."

I gave Mike a slight nod, knelt beside Melissa, and leaned over to her ear. "It's okay, love. We'll be fine. Go and be with the Lord."

A few minutes later our mothers started to sing. Suddenly Melissa sat straight up in her bed and put her hands on their mouths, as if she was saying, "No, I'm not going yet!" She became restless, fidgeting in the bed. We all began praying. Melissa tugged at her legs and told us to lower the bed rails because she wanted to get up.

We told her that we couldn't, but then we all seemed to realize that God might be healing her, and we quickly let the rails down. Melissa swung her legs out of the bed, stood up, and looked me directly in the eyes.

"It's gone," she said. "It's gone!"

I didn't know how to respond.

"Jeremy, you have to believe me. It's all gone!"

Confused, I asked what she meant. "Are you healed?"

"Yes," she answered. "It's all gone."

The room instantly broke out in rejoicing. I hugged Melissa. My brother Jared embraced both of us. Our mothers started jumping up and down and hugging each other too. We all continued to rejoice and thank God for her healing.

Melissa lunged, trying to walk, and would have fallen if a friend hadn't caught her. She said she needed to go into the restroom. We told her that she couldn't just yet because of all the tubes hooked up to her, so she would have to wait. We helped her back into bed, and she lay back with the most peaceful look on her face.

I went outside the room and started calling friends to tell them what had just happened. "I think maybe God healed her."

Melissa slept off and on that day, sitting up and talking at times. There was a glazed look in her eyes that we assumed was caused by all the medication. We hoped she would be back to her old self again as soon as the medication wore off. A renewed level of energy filled the room.

When she was awake and speaking, we'd talk to her for as long as we could before she drifted back to sleep. When she was asleep, I'd go out into the hallway or take a walk and marvel at the possibility that my Melissa had been healed.

But over the span of a few hours she became more unresponsive again. Her vital signs became poor and she appeared even weaker than before.

I was confused. Was she healed or not? I returned to the waiting room next door, drained. Lying facedown on the floor, I cried aloud, "Lord, what is happening?"

I stayed on the floor, weeping and crying out to God for answers.

Then, sensing someone else's presence, I looked to see a friend standing in the doorway.

"Jeremy," he said in a somber tone, "it's time."

I got off the floor and started what seemed like a long walk to her room. My brother and parents walked with me.

Jared, with a hurt look in his eyes, stopped and hugged me. He cried as we embraced. "It's not over," Jared said. "She's not gone yet."

We took a couple of steps toward Melissa's room when, for some reason, it struck me: Jared, barely a teenager, was maturing spiritually, and this could be a hinge moment for his faith in God. I wanted to give him reassurance for his walk with Christ.

I grabbed Jared and looked at him face-to-face.

"Whatever you do," I told him, "don't you ever stop serving Jesus. Just because we live in a sick, sin-filled world doesn't mean He's not in control."

Jared nodded.

I could feel my legs buckling as I walked into Melissa's room. Other than worship music playing from a CD player, the room was quiet. I approached Melissa and fell beside her onto the bed. I hugged her. "I love you," I said.

At 12:05 a.m. on Monday, February 5, 2001, Heather whispered, "She's with Jesus now."

I rolled out of the bed and onto the floor, where I curled into a ball. Melissa's family began worshipping the Lord, raising their hands and singing along with the CD. Then my mom started singing, followed by my dad and other members of our families.

I had no desire to sing. I just wanted to stay in my spot on the floor and cry.

But then God spoke into my heart: *I want you to stand up and worship Me.*

Oh, God, no! I don't want to stand up and worship right now. There's nothing in me that can do that!

My mom, in a mother's tender but firm voice, told me, "Honey, you have to lift your hands, you have to worship the Lord."

I knew that I *had* to trust God, that even in the most painful and crushing times, He is still worthy to be praised. I slowly rose to my knees, and then my parents helped me to my feet. I began singing and lifted my hands alongside the others around Melissa's bed.

I had never felt God's presence as powerfully as I felt it then. Melissa's body lay lifeless in front of us, but I knew that her soul was worshipping her Lord and Savior. She was in the presence of her King—pain-free and no longer suffering.

The journey had been long for all of us. It had drained us physically and emotionally. I didn't think I had the strength to walk on my own, so I put my arms around my dad and a close friend, and they helped me leave Melissa's room.

Time to Trust

When I woke up at our apartment later that morning, my first thought was, *I'm going to get a phone call telling me she's been healed—that she's alive.* I told my mom, and she said she'd had a similar thought.

We had so much faith that Melissa would be healed, latching

on to scriptures filled with promises that we believed meant healing would come to her.

Shortly after Melissa had stood beside her hospital bed and declared, "It's gone! It's gone!" her brother, Ryan, had asked me whether I believed God had healed her. I don't remember the exact words of his next question, but I do clearly remember its essence: God wouldn't be so cruel to give us false hope that she had been healed, would He?

"No way, man," I had answered Ryan.

But then Melissa lay back in the bed and never got up again. "Why would You do that?" I asked God. "Why would You give us that hope? Why did You let us have that hope about having kids? We started talking about having kids, and then obviously we were supposed to have kids because she didn't have to have the hysterectomy."

I sensed God telling me, "I gave you that hope because I didn't want you going into your marriage right away thinking that you weren't going to have kids."

I kind of understood that.

But then I asked, "Why would she say she had been healed? Why would You let that happen?"

The realization began to set in that perhaps she was indeed being healed at that moment—a different type of healing from what I had been praying for, believing for, and hoping for, but healed the way God wanted. I believed that God had been revealing to Melissa that the cancer and all the pain and suffering was being removed from her as she entered His presence for eternity.

But still, I struggled with the fact that I had believed that Melissa would be healed here on this earth.

There's a simple word for what I had to do at that time: *trust*.

Chapter 12

WHY?

What do you do when your best option is to trust someone, but at that point in your life you don't fully have the ability to trust? And what if you've learned that just because you trust God doesn't mean that everything is safe, that nothing bad will happen?

That confusing place is where I was with God after Melissa went to heaven. After the memorial service, I returned to Indiana to spend time with my family. I just needed to get away from our apartment and the West Coast and all their daily reminders of Melissa.

Melissa and I hadn't really even had the chance to establish our new normal after the wedding, and barely more than a hundred days since we had said "until death do us part," I wasn't prepared to start my new, new normal apart from her. I was a twenty-three-year-old widower. That last word was difficult to come to grips with.

Numb is the closest word to describe how I felt. Getting out of bed in the mornings seemed to require full effort. If I could have stayed in bed and pulled the covers over my head to avoid confronting my confusion, I would have. But the confusion would have crept under the covers. It was everywhere I turned.

It wasn't like I suddenly stopped knowing all the good things about God that I have mentioned to this point in the book. I was thankful God had brought Melissa into my life. I was grateful for the strength He had given me, which was the only reason I had been able to make it through the difficult circumstances. I wanted to trust God—I knew I needed to trust Him—but because I had believed He would heal Melissa and He didn't do so the way I believed He would, my trust in Him was hindered.

I was taking my questions directly to God, but there didn't seem to be a solid connection between us. It was like when you are talking with someone on a cell phone, you enter a bad cell, and the conversation starts breaking up. You know the other person is on the line with you and talking to you, but you're not able to receive the message. Except that I had been in that bad cell for two weeks and was beginning to wonder if God and I would ever communicate like we had before.

So that's why I was a little surprised to sense God telling me *Pick up your guitar* on the day I was sitting alone on my parents' couch. First, I was surprised because I had sensed those words clearly. Second, I didn't feel like I had anything to offer God, or anyone for that matter, physically or emotionally. Imagine a tire with all its air leaked out. It's still a tire, but without air it's useless. I felt like that tire.

After resisting God's urging for perhaps half an hour, I picked up my guitar. Ten minutes later, "I Still Believe" was completed.

There was no thought of, *This is going to be a big hit song.* The purpose of that song was so I could be ministered to, and all I've done in the years since is share it with others.

I sat back on the couch and sighed. In the middle of all my confusion, I felt God's presence. In the middle of my pain, I felt His grace and sensed His mercy.

That song made some big statements for me. It was from the Bible that I had taken what I believed to be promises that Melissa would be healed, but in the song I said that I still believed in God's holy Word. That I believed in His truth. That I believed in His faithfulness.

Through those words written from my soul, I was saying, "You are faithful. You are faithful. You are faithful." Even in all the hardships, I still believed. I did fully trust Him!

That moment is what I look back to now as the beginning of my heart's healing.

Obedience to God can result in dramatic change, even though in my case it wasn't the most tenderhearted obedience. Obedience opens our heart's door to allow God to do the work He desires.

"Do You Believe This?"

Being in Indiana was good for me because while in the same house with my parents, they shared their wisdom with me. Though grieving themselves, they still spoke words of comfort and healing.

As always, my mom seemed to know the exact words from the Bible that I needed to hear. Each day—sometimes multiple times per day—she would share a verse with me that she felt the Lord had placed on her heart to speak to my situation.

My mom found comfort herself in Hebrews 11. The first verse gives us the definition of faith many of us memorized as youngsters: "Now faith is the substance of things hoped for, the evidence of things not seen" (KJV). The chapter also includes the members of the "Hall of Faith"—heroes and heroines of the Old Testament who serve as examples to us because they remained strong in their faith although they did not see certain promises from God fulfilled in their lifetimes.

My mom pointed me to the final two verses that wrap up that chapter, verses 39 and 40: "These were all commended for their faith, yet none of them received what had been promised, since God had planned something better for us so that only together with us would they be made perfect."

"I don't understand why God gave us those promises," she told me, "but I feel like He's telling us that though we were given the promises, we didn't receive what had been promised, but we were to walk by faith. And this would be a deeper kind of faith."

There were several occasions in my parents' house when my dad would walk up to me and just hug me and hold me tight while I cried. There was a time when we were singing worship songs together and I had to stop. "She was such a worshipper," I told my dad and started crying. My dad reached over and embraced me without saying a word. My dad was great about just letting me cry when I wanted to. I am blessed to have a father who loves God and loves me with the tenderness he has shown me.

Early in the spring of 2001, I returned to California. I wasn't convinced I was ready to live there without Melissa, but I felt that was where God wanted me to be. It wasn't easy being there because there were visual reminders of Melissa everywhere—the restaurants where we ate, the places we hung out, the church we attended. My friends weren't only my friends, but they were our friends.

I didn't want to live in our apartment alone, so Melissa's brother, Ryan, and another friend both stayed with me for a while at different points.

Being in our apartment was especially emotional. Melissa loved Thomas Kinkade paintings, and two of his prints that we had picked out together hung on our walls—one a gift from Kinkade himself, another I bought for her. I would be in the kitchen dicing carrots and start crying at the memory of juicing carrots in hopes that would help her beat the cancer. I would sit in bed and watch TV and think of how she used to be there right next to me. But then I would remember that stinking monitor with the bag and the tube and the beeping noise that would wake me up in the middle of the night to keep the fluids flowing through her.

There was just a crazy amount and mix of emotions.

The numbness I felt immediately after Melissa's death turned to sadness. After a while, the sadness gave way to anger. I was angry over her life ending far too soon. She was only twenty-one with so much to offer! I was angry that so many hopes and dreams were snatched from us so suddenly.

One day I was reading the Bible in my bedroom when I came across a passage in which Jesus miraculously healed someone. I couldn't even finish the passage because it felt like a volcano had been awakened inside me. I stood, picked up my Bible, and flung it across the room. It slammed against the wall and fell to the floor. "Why Lord?! Why didn't You heal my wife? I had faith! I believed! *Why?!*"

I'm not prone to angry eruptions like that, and the anger I felt wasn't constant. I just had moments when I would think about everything that had happened and become upset. But I had tried to hold back my feelings of anger toward God because I had told myself that He was God, and I couldn't be angry at God. I had asked Him a lot of questions, but I hadn't wanted to actually question *Him*. That seemed like a line I couldn't—and shouldn't—cross. Yet there was such a wide-ranging mix of emotions pent up within me that it had become more than I could hold back.

My pulse had quickened. My lungs were working overtime. I could feel how tense my muscles had become, and I wanted to punch a hole in the nearest wall. I was a little freaked out about how I had responded—*You threw your Bible!* I reminded myself—and took a few deep breaths to settle down my body.

Again, I sensed the Lord placing words in my heart: "You're not supposed to know why. That is not My purpose for you. I want you to have a testimony of walking by faith."

That was not what I wanted to hear, but I calmed down even though I still didn't fully understand.

Another day when I was reading the Bible, God directed me to spend time studying the story of Lazarus in John 11. Lazarus was sick and dying in Bethany. Mary and Martha, Lazarus's sisters and friends of Jesus, called for Jesus because they knew He could heal Lazarus. Jesus was less than two miles away in Jerusalem when Mary and Martha's request was delivered. Yet instead of dropping everything and rushing off to Bethany, Jesus remained in Jerusalem. By the time Jesus did arrive in Bethany, Lazarus had died and had been in the tomb for four days. Mary and Martha had been dealing with mourners and well-wishers all that time before Jesus showed up for the first time. Martha heard Jesus was coming and went out to meet Him. As I read through the story, I didn't have to imagine Martha's hurt, confusion, and anger.

In verse 21, she said to Jesus, "If you had been here, my brother would not have died."

In verses 25–26, Jesus reminded her, "I am the resurrection and the life. The one who believes in me will live, even though they die; and whoever lives by believing in me will never die." Then He asked Martha a direct question: "Do you believe this?"

Do you believe this?

Martha's question to answer was mine to answer too. Did I believe that the Lord was willing to heal? I had been wrestling with that question every hour of every day. Would I continue to believe that Jesus was the resurrection and the life? And that Melissa was more "alive" now than she had ever been on earth?

Later in the story of Lazarus, it is revealed that it wasn't because of callousness or indifference that Jesus hadn't come sooner. As "God made man," Jesus felt every emotion we could ever feel. He loved, He rejoiced, He felt anger (just ask the money changers in the temple[10]), and, of course, He suffered.

Verse 35 is another scripture many of us memorized at an early age because, as the shortest verse in the Bible, it was the easiest to learn: "Jesus wept." It's also one of the most profound verses in God's Word because it demonstrates the true empathy of our Savior.

Jesus didn't merely cry; the original word translated "wept" basically means convulsing out of a depth of sorrow that shakes one to the core of his or her being. A person probably could not be more overcome with mourning than Jesus was.

Fully God and fully man, Jesus had to know the end result in Lazarus's death—that he would walk out of the tomb a risen man. Why did Jesus mourn so? I think one big reason is that Jesus loved Lazarus, and He loved Mary and Martha, so He knew how much they were hurting. I believe He empathized with the sisters' pain as they grieved the death of their brother.

After all, He had done the same with me. I could feel Him weeping with me at times. Whether I was hurting, confused, angry, or questioning Him, the Lord never withdrew from me. When I had expressed my anger by throwing my Bible, God already knew how I felt. He already knew my thoughts. My actions were merely me being myself.

Recognizing the Lord's continuous presence didn't eliminate my battles and struggles. My hard questions weren't erased. I *still* asked them. In fact, I still have some I ask. But that day when I studied the story of Lazarus, I acquired a sense of peace in knowing that I was not alone—that my Savior was with me.

A Big Step Forward

My parents had encouraged me to reach out to Jon Courson. I had not talked with anyone who had been through anything similar to me, but Jon's wife had been killed in a car accident, leaving him with three children. Then later, a teenage daughter died in another car accident.

When I made contact with Jon, he graciously invited Melissa's brother and me to visit him in Oregon.

Ryan and I didn't have schedules to worry about, so we decided to turn the visit into a road trip. We stopped wherever we wanted on our way up the coast. We would decide to get off the main road on a whim and look for fun things to do. At one stop, we found a creek and decided to jump in and swim for a while. Then we got out and sat next to the creek and just talked.

Ryan was a rad dude, and that time was important for us to spend together. We experienced ups and downs on the trip. We would be laughing and joking around or doing something fun, then one of us would think about Melissa and a switch would flip. Our conversation would turn somber, and we would cry as we reminisced about Melissa and talked about how much we missed her.

As we neared our destination, I felt a mix of anticipation and uncertainty. I hoped Jon would be able to answer my questions about Melissa's death—and I had plenty of questions to ask him—yet I also realized that talking with Jon would smash against some of the raw emotions I still carried. Plus, I felt a bit of uneasiness at what those answers might be. Could I handle whatever answers he would offer?

As much as my family and friends had carried me through my difficult times, I could tell when we greeted Jon that he could relate to me in a way no other person had. He was so warm in welcoming us and putting us up in a small cabin on his property.

Anyone who has heard Jon speak knows he has a deliberate, fatherlike delivery when he talks—and he has a fatherlike personality to match his voice. He comes across almost like a Santa Claus. I could have closed my eyes and imagined Jon in a red suit and white beard, saying to me, "Ho, ho, ho. Come here, son."

After Ryan and I unpacked, we met with Jon for our first discussion. One of my first questions dealt with Melissa's suffering.

"There was so much pain," I said. "What about that? Why did

she have to suffer like that? She loved the Lord. We did everything we could. We prayed, we believed. I just don't understand it."

Jon answered with wise words I have not forgotten. He began by asking me a series of questions:

"Did you do all the things God's Word says to do?"

"Did you fast and pray?"

"Did you have the elders come and pray and anoint with oil?"

"Did you believe?"

"Did you have faith?"

I answered yes to each. We all had done all those things up until her final breath.

"Jeremy," he then said, "you can rest your head on your pillow at night, knowing you did all that you could. That was God's plan. He heard your prayers. He comforted Melissa. Rest, knowing that you did seek the Lord in obedience."

Later in the conversation, Jon used the story of Miriam—the sister of Moses and Aaron—from Exodus 14–15 as an illustration. "Remember after the Israelites crossed the Red Sea, and Miriam was playing her song of celebration on the tambourine?"

"Yes," I answered and imagined Miriam dancing and praising after the Hebrews had safely reached the other side of the Red Sea, removed from the threat of the Egyptian army.

"Well," Jon continued, "she missed out on the depths of how God could have used her."

I had always pictured Miriam as a heroine in the story. "Missed out?" I asked. "What do you mean?"

"What she did, she really should have done earlier," Jon explained. "Granted, I wasn't there, but when they were all assembled *before* crossing the Red Sea, not knowing what to do, she could have been singing and praising the Lord on that side as well—not just afterward."

Imagine if Miriam had pulled out a tambourine and started dancing and praising the Lord when the Israelites were trapped between the

Red Sea and the Egyptian army, when everyone around her was terrified because of the circumstances. Miriam's friends probably would have thought there were a few zils loose in her tambourine, if you know what I mean.

But what Miriam missed out on was experiencing the fullness of how God could have used her in a greater capacity. God didn't suddenly become good *after* they crossed the Red Sea. Twenty-twenty hindsight revealed that God was good, too, when the Israelites were trapped with seemingly no way out because He had a plan all along to bring them out—to rescue them—in a way they never could have imagined. And Miriam missed out on an opportunity to glorify God in the midst of an uncertain and unsettling situation.

Jon brought the story of Miriam into the here and now by reminding me that we still should worship God in our difficult circumstances—that He is worthy of being worshipped in our difficult circumstances.

"He's still in control," Jon told me. "It's easy *after* we've tasted God's deliverance and seen His miracles to say, 'Yes, Lord, You are the best!' But it's tough when you don't see any outcome or any good in a really dark time to say, 'God, You are good. You are good. No matter what, You are good.'"

That was so much easier to hear when we were talking about Miriam instead of me. The last thing I felt like doing in the wake of Melissa's death was saying, "Yeah, Lord—You're good! You are good!" I mean, when we lost football games in high school, none of us cheered. The coach didn't tell us, "Hey, you lost—go celebrate with your teammates."

But that football analogy is admittedly shortsighted. In my life, there was a much larger picture than what I could see because of the circumstances around me. I might have felt like I was walking off the field after the end of a game, but if I stepped back and looked at my life from the perspective of eternity—from God's perspective—I was barely starting to break a sweat in pregame warm-ups. Our time here on earth can seem like everything to us, but in reality it's only a miniscule part of the plan that God is working. Our time here is to prepare us for our eternity with Him.

I needed that eternal perspective Jon was bringing to me. "We'll probably never fully understand suffering," he said, "until we're in the presence of the Lord for eternity."

Jon used the illustration of a caterpillar to help Ryan and me better understand the concept of suffering. A caterpillar struggles to get out of its cocoon. The temptation would be to help free the caterpillar, but the pressure of the struggle is what allows it to develop into a butterfly. If the caterpillar were to be removed prematurely from the struggle, it would not properly develop and would die. The caterpillar's struggle is what allows a butterfly to become what it is created to be.

Likewise, the "beauty" of our lives often is the result of a season of struggle. Through our struggles, we gain strength and maturity. We want God to remove us from our struggles, but what would it be like if He did as we desired? We would be weak and immature! That's not what God created us to be. Unfortunately for us sometimes, strength and maturity arise only out of pain. We can wish there was an easier way, but the results are undeniable.

"I know it doesn't make sense," Jon said, "but pain is a part of the bigger picture. Through the suffering, God works toward a greater purpose. In heaven now, Melissa's reward is great. If we can look at things from an eternal perspective, we can see that her reward is so much greater than any earthly suffering."

I knew that was true, but still it was difficult to grasp because we have earthly mind-sets and we can only comprehend the things we know. We can imagine what God's Word describes about heaven, but the fact is we don't know much about what heaven is like. Our earthly minds limit us. I needed to learn all I could about heaven from

Scripture and trust God that Melissa was in a better place, a place where she didn't suffer. In Colossians 3:2, Paul wrote, "Set your minds on things above, not on earthly things." Again, I needed that type of eternal perspective.

Jon invited me to play a song at his church's Sunday night service. I was honored but hesitant. I didn't feel like I was in a state in which I could be used by God.

At Melissa's graveside, my good friend Jean-Luc had told me, "Let's hasten the day!" He would tell me several times later, "Don't give up! Let's hasten the day! Let's tell more people about Jesus so that He will come quicker!"

It sounded good when Jean-Luc would say that, and it would spur me on to realize that I still had a lot of ministering to do for others ahead of me. But the timing didn't seem right yet. I thought I had issues to get squared away in my heart—questions that needed to be answered—before God could use me.

Jon, though, wanted me to see how I could be used by God—that night.

"I think it will be good for you," he said, "because at your greatest depth of pain, God will use you to have the greatest impact."

I was at my greatest depth of pain, so if Jon was correct, then I certainly was at the point where I could be used for the greatest impact.

I chose to play and sing "I Still Believe." It was the first time I had performed the song publicly. I mostly cried my way through the song and then briefly shared about Melissa's passing. I don't even remember what I told the congregation, but I do recall all the compassion I saw on the faces of the people and how many were wiping tears. Singing the song and talking about Melissa was painful but powerful. I felt like, instead of standing on a platform, I was standing in God's hands because He was the One who was holding me up. I didn't feel really strong, but I recognized that all the strength I did have was coming from God.

Afterward, members of the congregation came up to me and hugged me, prayed for me, offered me encouraging words, and told me how the song and story had spoken to them. It was a sweet moment, and I left the church that night amazed at how God had ministered both to my pain and through my pain.

While I talked with Jon over a couple of days, the fog I was in didn't dramatically lift to reveal everything I wanted to see in my time of trials. But thanks to the truth Jon was lovingly speaking to me, I did think I was beginning to see better than before.

I left Oregon with a glimmer of hope, and that was a lot more hope than I had when I had arrived. I left with a little bit more resolve because I noted how Jon had been through two tragedies—the deaths of his wife and a daughter—and he seemed to be doing fine, and he was able to use his difficult times to minister to people. I left finally beginning to think, *It's gonna be okay.*

Chapter 13

BREAKING THROUGH

The resolve in my heart had begun with the writing of "I Still Believe." Now, I felt like the resolve was moving into the action stage.

After the trip to Oregon, I was ready to go out and play and sing. I wanted to share "I Still Believe," Melissa's story, and what God had done and was doing in my life. That spring and into the summer, as I sang and shared and as congregations responded, I began to receive more invitations to sing or lead worship in churches.

It was odd, but there were two contrasting trends at work. On one hand, I would find myself telling God before a service, "Lord, I don't *feel* like worshipping You today. I don't *feel* like saying 'I still believe.'" I knew the words were true, but they didn't feel true. But on the other hand, even though at times I felt like a reluctant participant, I could feel God's presence as I sang, and there was a greater impact on audiences than I could have anticipated. I could see and feel that God was moving among people, and I knew it had nothing to do with me because only a few minutes earlier I had been telling God I didn't want to sing that song. Again, I learned a valuable lesson about the importance of obedience over feelings.

When I would lead worship, I noticed myself paying more attention than before to the lyrics. Every lyric seemed to mean something to me. Every lyric was an opportunity for me to explore the depths of God's love and grace, and I was understanding things about the nature of God that I probably wouldn't have even considered before. I still had my share of ups and downs. I still had some really rough days. Different triggers could unexpectedly unleash an angry river of emotions.

Seeing a young couple holding hands in a park would make me miss Melissa. Seeing a mom and dad playing with their child at a park would make me think that could have been Melissa and me and our kid—even sometimes that it *should* have been our family. I cried in a theater during a scene of grief in a war movie.

The triggers were potentially everywhere, and because I didn't know when they would pop up, I couldn't always keep myself protected from them.

I felt myself becoming angry too easily. I saw a couple at a restaurant, and I could tell from their mannerisms that they were having some type of disagreement. I got mad at the guy and wanted to go tell him, "Come on—appreciate your wife!"

I lost the compassion for others I had felt beginning back at Bible college. Instead, I judged others as being selfish. After all, their problems they were so concerned about were nothing compared to mine! I was mad at the world and ready to take it on. Me against the world—let's do this!

But at the same time, my music career was on an upswing. It was a crazy roller-coaster ride I was on, experiencing ups and downs seemingly at the same time. When I was singing or leading worship, I could put the anger aside temporarily.

Friends lovingly told me they were concerned that it might be too soon for me to jump back into music ministry. I understood why they were saying that. If I had been them and saw me in the condition I was in, I might have said the same thing. I *was* still grieving. But I honestly believed that God was gently nudging me back into music ministry, saying, *I'll take care of you. You just go ahead, walk into what I'm doing.* Writing songs from my heart and then sharing them was an important part not only of my healing but also of encouraging and offering hope to others.

I was witnessing incredible responses when I sang "I Still Believe" and "Walk by Faith," and recording them would create a much wider area for them to make an impact. A friend told me about two young producers, Adam Watts and Andy Dodd. I listened to some of their work, liked it, and called them to ask about the possibility of recording a demo.

"It's a hard time in my life," I told them, "but I need to get these songs out." Adam and Andy agreed without hesitation. We recorded "Walk by Faith" first. When we were in the studio working on the final mixes of the song, I had a strong feeling that God was going to use the song to provide hope and encouragement to many people suffering through painful trials.

"Thank You, Lord," I prayed, "that You might use what Melissa and I have gone through to help others in their own struggles."

I felt a sense of excitement over knowing that God had big things in store for my future, but I also knew that I wasn't fully prepared for the next step. Specifically, my heart wasn't prepared. I had to allow God to eliminate the anger. I couldn't get so caught up in the idea that God was going to use one of my songs to minister deeply that I resisted the deep ministry He needed to accomplish in me.

Mission: Breakthrough

I scheduled a fall retreat to a one-room cabin in the mountains. I wanted one thing from the trip: a breakthrough. I felt God was about to do something big, and I didn't want to miss it.

I asked God to completely purge every ounce of coldness and bitterness from my heart. I remembered from my past where coldness and bitterness had gotten me before, and I didn't want to go there again. I needed God to give me a heart like He had given me back in Bible college. I wanted to be compassionate toward people again.

I had planned to stay in the small cabin three days, praying, fasting, and playing my guitar. It proved more difficult than I anticipated. Time passed slowly. Time didn't just crawl—sometimes it decided to stand still. I expected a big revelation to come down on me like an eagle majestically descending onto a high perch. I thought that, alone in the mountains with no distractions, I would hear God's voice and undergo an immediate and life-changing transformation. I was prepared to cry until I ran out of tears.

But there were no tears. There was still, however, plenty of coldness and bitterness. My mind and heart seemed stuck in gear. I just couldn't get past the same old questions and confusion. About the only thing I had picked up in the cabin was hunger pangs.

Then one of the times when I was messing around on my guitar, from out of my funk, a tune and words started coming to me that became the song "Breaking My Fall":

(Verse 1)
So easily I fall, so easily You reach Your hand out
Quickly will I drown, in all the pools of all my reason
So easily will I fear, so easily will Your peace surpass me
Quickly will I trust, in anything I think is worthy
How many times You make the waves calm down so I won't be
    afraid now

[Chorus]
I saw You breaking my, breaking my fall
What am I supposed to do?
'Cause I saw You breaking my, breaking my fall
What am I supposed to do?

(Verse 2)
How precious are Your thoughts, the many that You think
 about me
Faithful are Your ways, I always feel Your grace abounding
Quickly will I call, quickly will You answer my cry
Carefully will You bring, everything I need in my life
How many times You make the waves calm down
So I won't be afraid now

[Bridge]
This narrow road I'm walking, this world will try to draw
Your Word will help me fight it, with You I'll face it all[11]

The song's main question is "What am I supposed to do?" That's
the question I was asking in that cabin. I had gone there for a complete
breakthrough, but I didn't think I had even taken a step in the right
direction, much less had a breakthrough.

What was I supposed to do?

The song, though, did express my faith that somehow, some way,
God would deliver me from my pain: "Quickly will I call, quickly will
You answer my cry."

The problem was that God and I had different definitions of
quickly.

But I could see in the words that God was saying to me, "Hey,
I'm still here—even when you're stumbling. I love you. I'm thinking
about you. I am here."

In the time at my parents' home after Melissa's death, I had
struggled to clearly communicate with God. It was different in the
cabin, though, because I did feel a strong connection. I just wasn't
receiving the full breaking of my heart I had wanted.

"Lord, I want this!" I said at one point. "I'm falling and stumbling
and getting bitter and angry, but I'm fighting through to get this!"

I felt as though the Lord was responding, "I know that you're calling out to Me, and I'm telling you that I am breaking your fall. I'm thinking about you more than the sands of the sea."

On the third and final morning, I left the cabin disappointed my expectations hadn't been met. It certainly hadn't been a relaxing getaway in the mountains. I hadn't eaten much, and I hadn't slept much. I felt like I had been on the losing end of a long boxing match.

"Lord," I prayed, "my heart's desire was to have a huge revelation, weeping in Your presence, feeling Your healing touch—something momentous. I don't understand why nothing has changed." After eating at a restaurant near the cabin, I started down the mountain and toward home. The demo CD I'd recorded was in the car, and I slipped it into the player to hear how it sounded. As "Walk by Faith" played and I listened to the words God had given me on our honeymoon, the eagle landed on the perch.

Warmth penetrated my heart, melting the ice that had built up. All the pent-up emotions suddenly released. The floodgates to my eyes burst open. I came to a stop sign at an intersection and pulled over to the side of the road and buried my head in my hands.

As moving an experience writing "Walk by Faith" had been and as many times I had sung the song and meditated on the words, I had never fully grasped exactly what the song was saying until that moment on the side of the mountain road.

"Okay, Lord," I said aloud in the driver's seat. "I can't see, but I *will* walk by faith. I don't understand, but I know there's a greater plan. It will be okay—*You* will make it okay!"

I had been broken before, so I knew how it felt. And I knew I had just been broken again. What a relief! I remember being so thankful.

"I'm sorry, Lord, for being so upset," I said. "I get it now."

I had experienced several monumental moments in my life, when God had broken me down or spoken to me in a powerful way: the summer youth camp, in the chapel at Bible college, when I wrote "I Still Believe," my time with Jon Courson. That brief time beside a mountain highway was another of those moments. As I look back now, I recognize that time was the ultimate turning point in my processing what had happened to Melissa. I still encountered battles—and still do—but starting immediately at that point, everything changed.

I pulled back onto the highway and resumed my drive home. I continued talking to the Lord as I drove down the mountain, but the conversation had a drastically different tone—or at least the tone on my end of the conversation had changed.

Everything around me just seemed so peaceful. I had hope again. I could see the mountains around me again, and they were beautiful.

That was probably the quickest two-hour drive I've ever made in my life. I returned home a different man. The steps of healing that followed grew closer and closer together than they had been. Hope and expectancy characterized my prayer life. "Here I am, God—let's do this!" I would pray. "It's time to live. I'm broken, but whatever You want me to do, I'm willing."

Signing Up

In December 2001, I received an e-mail from Tyson Paoletti, a record-company representative at BEC Recordings.

"We've been hearing a lot about you from a friend," Tyson wrote, "and we would like to talk with you. Do you have a demo you could send?"

You bet I had a demo I could send!

I knew that Brandon Ebel was the head of BEC—which stood for Brandon Ebel Company—and when I was a teenager, my family had gotten to know him and camped next to him two or three times at the Cornerstone music festivals. I made sure to let Tyson know that.

A few days after I sent my six-song demo CD, Brandon called me. "Bro, what's going on?" he asked. "How is your family in Indiana?"

I told him my family was doing well and began to tell him about Melissa. I could tell by his reactions from the other end of the line that he was shocked. He expressed his condolences, and then paused.

"These songs—oh my goodness," he said. "There is a lot here. I'd really like to work with you."

As excited as I was, I told Brandon I couldn't give him an answer yet.

"I need to pray about this," I said. "I've been through a lot, and I need to make sure every decision is from God." Brandon told me to take all the time I needed.

Brandon and I stayed in contact, and one day he asked about my interest in recording an album as part of a yearly worship project called *Any Given Sunday.* That opportunity really interested me because I loved leading worship. Plus, several people had suggested that I make a recording of songs I had written—I had some more congregational-style songs that were personal about what God had done in my life—along with some of the popular worship songs I led in churches that were written by others.

I prayed about that in addition to the opportunity with BEC and felt God giving me the go-ahead on *Any Given Sunday.*

While we were working on the worship project, I felt a strong confirmation about signing a contract with BEC. Recording contracts are much more involved than people outside of the music industry realize.

To give a simple overview, when a singer-songwriter signs a contract, he signs over part ownership of the songs he writes for that particular label. The contract calls for the artist to record a certain number of songs for each CD, and the artist and label have to come to agreements regarding marketing and promotion of CDs and singles.

I haven't had a contract that required me to take part in concert tours, but artists understand that tours are part of the deal in terms of marketing and promotions. Labels invest money in artists, so the artists are expected to do their part to help sell CDs to pay off that investment. An artist who doesn't tour probably won't be re-signed by his or her label after recording the number of CDs established in the contract.

On top of all that, an artist and label have to come to terms on who gets what percentage of all the thises and thats in a contract. A longer, detailed description of recording contracts would probably give you a headache—if I haven't caused one already.

Jean-Luc, with his experience in the recording industry, was a big help. Even though I was sure that signing a contract was a part of God's plan for me, Jean-Luc wanted me to make sure I also made a good business decision. And I don't mind admitting that signing a contract to produce a certain number of CDs—to be filled with songs not yet written—can be a little scary. There were numerous times in the process of negotiating my first contract when I asked myself, *What if I run out of ideas for writing new songs?* After being in the industry for more than ten years, I haven't forgotten how Jean-Luc advised me in my early years, and I have tried to do the same with promising young artists getting started in the business. I know this concept bothers some people, but the reality is that ministry and business do intersect. Making good business decisions is an important part of being a good steward within ministry.

I had the *Any Given Sunday* project working—which later became *Carried Me: The Worship Project*—and then in May 2002, I signed a three-record contract with BEC.

I had been updating my parents throughout the contract-negotiating process, and they were the first phone call I made with the news: I officially was a signed artist!

Of course, they were excited. But my dad, as usual, told me: "I'm so proud of you because you're serving the Lord."

Signing the contract was such an amazing moment. I was stoked and ready to go. My personality type is such that, when it's time to begin something, I give it my all.

I was ready to go and do whatever the Lord wanted from me. I knew that He had opened that door for me—just as He had opened many doors previously to bring me to that spot—and I would be sharing the songs He had given me.

All right, Lord, I thought. *I fully know what You've done for me.*

Reaching Out

It's a good thing I had a "Let's do it!" mentality. After signing, I recorded two albums in about the span of a month.

Stay was the first CD released that September. The twelve songs included "Walk by Faith," "I Still Believe," and "Breaking My Fall." Five of the six songs on the demo I had sent to Tyson were a part of *Stay*. The other CD, *Carried Me: The Worship Project*, was released about a year and a half later and contained a mix of my songs and ones written by others.

Recording a CD can be physically and mentally taxing.

Recording two CDs in about a month—well, I'm not sure how to describe that. That was a crazy month, for sure, but my body and mind were energized from knowing my songs would be reaching more people than I had dreamed of reaching and would be offering them messages of encouragement and hope.

A big break for my career came with the invitation to participate in the forty-city Festival Con Dios tour, a traveling Christian music festival started the previous year by Newsboys. When I was officially booked to join the tour, I thanked God that He would be allowing me to share my music and testimony with so many people across the country.

The headliners of Festival Con Dios (Spanish for "Festival with

God") were Audio Adrenaline, TobyMac, MercyMe, and Out of Eden. Others on the tour included Pillar, The Benjamin Gate, Tree63, Sanctus Real, Everyday Sunday, and Aaron Spiro. I had been listening to those other artists—some for more years than they cared to hear when I informed them—and now I was sharing the same stage and ministering alongside them.

Festival Con Dios was so rad!

Six semitrucks carried a full-size stage, lights, and one hundred thousand watts' worth of sound equipment. The setup had room for about ten thousand people, who could bring folding chairs and blankets to sit on. The festival wasn't all about music, either. There was a "village" with merchandise tents, food vendors, bungee jumping, and other games that traveled with us. Plus, a professional motocross racer was part of the show and performed aerial stunts on his motorcycle.

Needless to say, there was a lot of energy involved in the tour. Right off the bat I got to taste the good life of touring because I was able to travel by bus. The less-glamorous side of touring includes traveling with a fifteen-passenger van and a trailer. The members of the band travel in a van—taking turns driving—and haul their equipment in a trailer hitched to the van. Some bands on the tour had to do the trailer-and-van routine.

But to start with, BEC told me, "We want you just to go and do what you're supposed to do," and they footed the bill for me to share a bus with another band. I sure enjoyed the "luxury" of the bus and felt bad for the trailer-and-van bands. If I had known then what I learned from my trailer-and-van experience on my first solo tour—when we played about 220 dates and were on the road for 300 days—I would have felt even worse for them and probably tried to make as much room as I could for them on our bus.

My band consisted of me, a guitar player, a bass player, and a drummer. We usually had about twenty minutes onstage at each of the stops. When I had made my onstage debut playing one song with The

Kry, I had been almost a nervous wreck. Starting out on Festival Con Dios was a little nerve-wracking when I thought about being onstage with my own band. But once I got onstage, I never found myself in "What do I do now?" mode because I was confident in what God had called me to do.

Stay released during Festival Con Dios, and with the tour and CD sales reaching a growing audience, Melissa's story and my testimony made an immediate connection with more fans. People wrote and e-mailed me, and fans came up to me on the tour to tell me their stories about their journeys with family members who had cancer. Others who had loved ones pass away told me how personal and meaningful the words of my songs were to them.

It was difficult to see and hear the pain in others' eyes and voices and words when they shared their stories, and there were emotional times around my merch table as fans would ask questions about my experiences and we would pray together. I loved the opportunities to have those conversations.

I knew how widespread cancer is, but I was blown away as I began to realize just how many people are directly impacted by the disease. But hearing and reading as many stories as I did confirmed a promise God had made to me in my most painful moments: He had a plan and a purpose for me that stretched far beyond anything I could have initially seen.

Chapter 14

FALLING IN
LOVE AGAIN

*S*tarting out with Festival Con Dios, I was in my element because with that many bands there were plenty of other musicians I could go up to and introduce myself. Why not? I was outgoing to begin with and excited to be touring with them.

At the beginning of the tour, as I had watched the other bands while I waited my turn, one particular artist had caught my eye and my ears: a red-haired girl with a big voice who was the front for The Benjamin Gate, or TBG for short.

TBG was a band from South Africa, and we had both played at Fish Fest in California earlier that summer, although I hadn't met them then. TBG also had been part of the first Festival Con Dios, and let me tell you, they could really rock it onstage. I assumed their lead singer—whose name, I asked and was told, was Adrienne Liesching, or Adie for short—was a loud and hard-core rocker chick.

After a show, while I was making the rounds of getting to know all the acts, I made my way over to Adrienne and introduced myself. She said hello in her South African accent, but it wasn't what I expected.

She wasn't anything like what she was onstage; she spoke with a soft and mellow tone.

Our first real conversation occurred after she had sprained an ankle in Atlanta, Georgia. The remnants of a tropical storm were pounding the area, and one of the tents looked like it was about to fly away in the storm. Our tour manager took off running to try to help save the tent and accidentally ran right into Adrienne. It looked like a well-executed tackle in a soccer match. Adrienne thought she was fine and told our tour manager to go help with the tent. But when she tried to stand up, she couldn't.

I felt bad for her because it's difficult for a rocker chick to rock onstage sporting an ankle brace. I saw Adrienne the next day and said, "We prayed for you today in our prayer before we went on." (Our band did pray for her—I promise!)

She thanked me, and as we talked, I kept noting how Adrienne actually had a quiet spirit about her. I almost had to make sure I was chatting with the same person I had watched onstage.

My merch table was two spots down from TBG's, and because Adrienne was their lead singer, she spent much of the day sitting at their table and meeting fans. I learned later that Adrienne had not yet heard me talk about Melissa onstage, but she had heard from her bandmates that I had an inspiring story she needed to check out. They had an entire conversation about my testimony in their van one day, and that had made Adrienne more intrigued.

Adrienne overheard some of the follow-up conversations about Melissa I was having with fans at my merch table, and during slow times around the tables, she would come over and say her soft "Hello" and ask me about Melissa. She would ask questions such as "What was she like?" or "How did you first meet?" or "Would you tell me about her walk with the Lord?" I liked how at ease Adrienne appeared to be talking about Melissa, and that made it easy to talk to her.

Other musicians would make mention of my testimony, but

Adrienne had a deeper interest in learning more than the others. She was really sweet about it. And it wasn't because she was attracted to me. She seemed to be intrigued by Melissa's and my story.

I'd see Adrienne out eating lunch or walk past her heading in the opposite direction, and I would acknowledge her with a "Hey, how's it going?" My band and her band would sit together sometimes while other groups were performing, and when TobyMac was doing his thing onstage, Adrienne and I would get up and dance all silly-like. She had done funky jazz dancing, growing up in South Africa, and she tried to teach me a few moves. We'd also do the "running man" hip-hop dance that MC Hammer and Vanilla Ice made popular during the late 1980s. I know Adrienne won't mind me saying this, but we basically were just being dorks. We were good friends, comfortable around each other, and not trying to impress the other.

Sometimes we would walk to our merch tables together and, because our tables were close to each other's, hang out in that area and just chat. She was so pleasant to talk with.

Adrienne was in a challenging spot. She was a young lady (twenty-one), far away from home, and traveling all the time with all dudes. She didn't seem to have anyone around her as a go-to person—that one person she could talk with about anything.

Iron sharpens iron, and she needed an iron-type person.[12]

Adrienne had a noticeable hunger for God. When she heard me talking about the Lord, she would ask questions about God just as she had asked questions about Melissa—in a personal and deeply interested way.

The more we got to know each other, the more our conversations focused on God and spiritual matters. Because I could see her desire to deepen her relationship with God, I felt comfortable challenging her gently and with the purpose of urging her to grow spiritually.

Adrienne had become disheartened by the Christian music scene. TBG had formed in South Africa in 1998 and had come to the United

States the year before I met her. They were in the middle of a stretch in which they did about 250 shows a year for three consecutive years, so they were grinding it trying to make it in the business. To make matters worse, they had been doing the van-and-trailer thing the entire time since moving to the States.

TBG was struggling a little, and Adrienne also felt like neither she nor the band was where they needed to be spiritually. Music no longer seemed to be worth the sacrifice it was requiring. Adrienne was becoming cynical. It was easy to understand why, but still, I didn't think she needed to be that way.

"You're jaded," I bluntly told her one day. I didn't duck when I said that, but I was unsure how she would receive my, um, attempting to sharpen her iron. But my intention was to speak the truth in love.

"Really?" she asked, partly wondering if she really was jaded and also, I think, partly put off by me telling her that.

"Yeah, absolutely you are. Don't be jaded. Don't have a hard heart because I know what that's like, and it's not good."

A few days later she thanked me for caring enough to notice and challenge her on her spiritual condition. She had been feeling distant from God, and He had been speaking to her heart that there was something not right in their relationship.

I felt like the Lord was bringing us together as close friends so that we could help each other work through the seasons we were going through in our respective lives.

We had some pretty personal conversations about Melissa.

Adrienne was curious. She asked a lot of questions, and I answered whatever she asked. Of course, I had talked to a ton of people about Melissa in the first few months after she passed away. But now, eight months removed from Melissa's death, Adrienne was the first woman I had talked to in depth about that time of my life, and it was beneficial for me to hear a woman's perspective.

Adrienne's band learned during the tour that a close friend back home in South Africa had been murdered, and I tried to comfort Adrienne the best I could based on my experiences with grief. There just seemed to be a lot going on in both of our lives, and our talks were producing healing for both of us.

I also was seeing the effectiveness I could have in one-on-one, personal conversations. I was getting used to talking about the example of Melissa's life onstage and with fans in an environment like the merch table, but something was different about doing so in depth with one person.

Despite the fact that we were spending more time with each other and having serious personal and spiritual conversations, there wasn't anything attraction-wise between us. Adrienne wasn't looking for someone, and I wasn't to the point yet of thinking about beginning another relationship.

On top of that, we weren't each other's type. I was the extroverted jock-type guy from the Midwest. Adrienne was the interesting mix of loud rocker/sweet introvert from South Africa. She was super artsy and creative, and I was, well, the jock-type guy.

We were nothing more than really, really good friends who had fun together, just as likely to sit down over lunch and talk about what we had read in the Bible that morning as we were to look at each other and say, "Wanna race?" then take off on a mad dash toward our imaginary finish line. (Except when she was in the ankle brace, although that didn't stop me from challenging her to a race.)

Adrienne had a small frame, and I had no idea she came from a family of good athletes. After her sprained ankle had healed, I threatened to dump a cup of cold water on her and she took off running. Let me tell you, I had to work to catch up with her. Needless to say, her sprinting ability impressed me.

What I liked most about Adrienne was how much she wanted to learn about God and just the curiosity level that would light up her face when we talked about spiritual matters.

Even though friendship was the full extent of our relationship, as we became closer, I started feeling guilty about spending so much time with her and then superguilty that I was having fun with a woman other than Melissa. I would wonder whether it was even okay for me to be friends with Adrienne.

I remember once, late in the fall of 2002, I was alone, and the guilt was weighing heavy on me. I said aloud, "Man, I can't do this."

I began to withdraw from Adrienne. We would cross paths, and I'd say, "Hey, good to see you! Sorry, but I've gotta go." I didn't tell Adrienne that I was intentionally backing away from her, but she told me later that she could tell that's what I was doing. She had told a friend she thought I was going to tell her we needed to stop spending time with each other.

The distance I was creating between us showed me how much I actually wanted to be around her. I would wonder what she was doing and then go out and try to "bump into her" somewhere around the tents. When I didn't find her, I would be disappointed. Every day, I felt more and more drawn to her. I missed her sweet spirit and playful personality. Our differences that I thought were proof we weren't each other's type? Perhaps, I began to consider, our relationship actually was a case of how opposites attract and complement each other.

But what I missed most was seeing her spiritual hunger. She had told me how Melissa inspired her and how she wanted to be "sold out for the Lord" like Melissa.

I realized that I liked Adrienne. And not merely liked but *liked*. Yes, that kind of like. And, although I didn't know it at the time, she was feeling the same way about me.

Adrienne thought I might like her, too, when a group of us were hanging out and playing pool and I let her beat me. I'm competitive, and in the spirit of good competition, I don't make a habit of losing on purpose.

But there was something different about Adrienne.

Going Our Separate Ways

"God," I prayed, "what's going on here? Being with Adrienne feels right and it doesn't feel right!"

"If I'm blessing you with something," He spoke to my heart, "don't question it too much. Receive My blessing."

I'd had enough of arguing with God in my prayers, so I quickly accepted His answer.

Then I remembered what Melissa had told me in that car ride home from the hospital: "I want to let you know that it's okay if you find somebody else after I go, and I don't want you to have to wait. You don't have to sit in this grief for a long time."

I hadn't wanted to hear those words then, and I didn't understand why Melissa would even say them when we still had so much to fight for. But suddenly, I recognized the stunning selflessness in her words and her wisdom in saying them even though it could not have been easy.

Growing closer to Adrienne was both exhilarating and frightening. After Melissa went to heaven, I put all my focus into ministering. That's all I wanted to do. I hadn't planned on falling in love again and hadn't seriously considered that one day I could.

When you lose a spouse to death, you become painfully aware of the great risk that comes with falling in love. I didn't really want to take that risk again, and that's one reason I had poured myself into ministry. Me and God—nobody else. No distractions. To a degree, nice and safe.

What's going on? I thought. *It's got to stop! I can't start another relationship. I don't even want to go there.*

I needed to break off our relationship before it advanced any further, so I asked Adrienne to dinner so I could tell her it was over. We went to an Applebee's in Oklahoma City, and I had a feeling that Adrienne knew what was coming. I knew what I needed to say, but I hadn't planned out how to say it.

We chitchatted a little, ordered our food, and chitchatted some more. The restaurant was busy, so it was fairly loud with all the conversations going on at the tables around us. All the while I was wondering how I was going to start off what I had to say.

Finally I decided I needed to do it before the food came. It wouldn't have been the best conversation to have between bites.

I looked across the table at her. She looked back at me.

"Can you imagine spending the rest of your life with me? I mean, do you feel like you could marry me?"

I'm not sure if Adrienne wanted to ask "What was that?" but I did! I couldn't believe I had just said that. That was the complete opposite of "Listen, I'm sorry, but this isn't right. I still want to be friends, but . . ."

Adrienne looked surprised but smiled. "Yes," she said.

"Okay," I said with a chuckle. "I've got to be honest—I came here tonight to kind of break it off with you. I've been feeling so much guilt and uncertainty. It's just overwhelming. But I couldn't. That's what came out. I've been through too much to play games, so—I hope you don't mind that I just asked you such a serious question."

"It's totally fine," she replied. "I'm glad we can just lay it all out like that."

The waiter brought our entrees, and both of us picked at our food more than we ate it. I think we did more sitting there and looking at each other and wondering if what we thought had just happened had actually happened.

Festival Con Dios concluded before Thanksgiving, and I did not want to be apart from Adrienne. When we went our separate ways, we really went our separate ways. Adrienne's band was based in Nashville, Tennessee, and I still lived in California. We compared our schedules and figured it would probably be at least a month before we would see each other again.

Thank goodness for cell phones! We talked practically every day, often for hours and sometimes until three or four o'clock in the

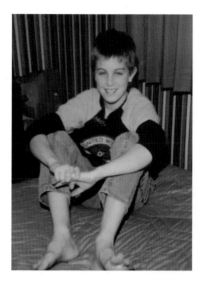

Me at seven years old

Camp family photo (L to R, back to front): April, me, Teri, Tom, Jared, and Josh

Me with my dad, Tom, and brothers, Jared and Josh

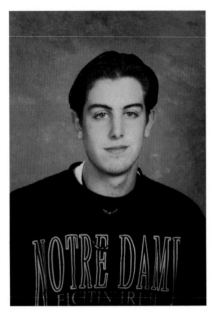

Freshman year

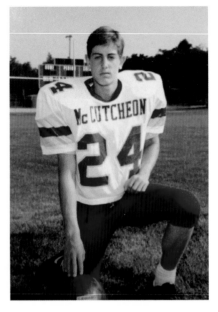

Freshman football
(being a football player
was my dream)

The Melissa I will always remember

Melissa and I, engaged 2000

October 21, 2000

Melissa and I in Hawaii on our honeymoon, October 2000

Four Gold records
(L to R: Mike Snider,
Matt Balm, me,
Brandon Ebel)

The same Power that rose Jesus
from the grave lives in us!

Tour rehearsal with my
manager, Matt Balm

At Dodger Stadium
with my band

Visiting Adrienne at one of her shows before we were married in 2003

December 15, 2003

Our family (L to R): Bella, me, Egan, Adrienne, Arie

On the red carpet with Adrienne, during the 50th GMA Dove Awards

Filming the "Dead Man Walking" music video

With Matt Balm in India, during a Speaking Louder Ministries outreach

With Bella and Arie at a Speaking Louder Ministries outreach in Uganda, 35,000 in attendance

Introducing "I Still Believe"
for the first time

At CinemaCon, Las Vegas,
introducing the movie *I Still
Believe* along with Lionsgate
and Kingdom Studios

The Camp family
with Britt Robertson
and KJ Apa, on set
of *I Still Believe*

From the *I Still
Believe* set

morning. Even over the phone, our talks were as deep as they had been in person. I would say we talked about everything, but that's probably too obvious because we would have to talk about everything to stay on the phone with each other as often and for as long as we did.

Three prominent topics for us were our relationships with the Lord, our future together, and my time with Melissa.

Adrienne stayed hungry to grow deeper in her relationship with God, and we had decided to read through the Bible together and then talk about the various things the Lord would highlight for us. I loved Adrienne's curiosity about all matters spiritual, and the questions she asked me made me feel like I was playing an important role in her spiritual growth. It was so obvious she was growing, and hearing the excitement in her voice as she recognized herself maturing spiritually made me want to be alongside her instead of having to settle for talking over the phone.

After the Applebee's conversation we had mutually understood that we possessed relationship possibilities that warranted further exploration. That's an English-class-essay way of saying that everything was totally rad between us and it was definitely "on." Those phone calls while we were separated were a time of getting to know each other better. Although we spent a lot of time together on the tour, we hadn't had many opportunities for extended one-on-one conversations. Because the tour basically was a traveling community, we spent most of our time hanging out in groups or with our bands. Once, I remember, Adrienne and I were able to sit down alone for about half an hour and have a good talk where we quizzed each other about everything we possibly could. We also took a few walks together, but at music festivals attended by thousands of people, they were far from long walks together in a serene rolling meadow.

So it wasn't until after the tour that we were able to enjoy uninterrupted time, even if it was all by phone. Every time we talked, I became more convinced that we needed to be together.

Talking with Adrienne about Melissa was such an important part of my healing process. I can't overstate how helpful and mature Adrienne was. She was the perfect example of a friend carrying another's burdens. I could talk to Adrienne about anything concerning Melissa, and she listened with such a sympathetic heart that there were many conversations that wound up with both of us crying.

During some of our discussions about Melissa, Adrienne would tell me, "I'm feeling a little insecure today." I appreciated her being honest in admitting that. It would have been easy for her to think, *This is my problem*, and keep it to herself. But her feelings of insecurity were something that we both needed to work through together. Her letting me know how she felt created opportunities for me to tell her that I didn't have any expectations for her to live up to in comparison to Melissa. In fact, I was very intentional about never comparing Adrienne to Melissa in any way. I would tell Adrienne that she and Melissa were different and then try to reassure Adrienne of her strengths.

Adrienne did one thing I especially appreciated when we talked about Melissa: she would ask me questions about Melissa's spiritual walk. Adrienne would tell me, based on what I had told her, how much she admired Melissa and how it sounded like Melissa had the type of relationship with the Lord that she was seeking. Talking about Melissa seemed beneficial for both of us, and that was important because it gave me the freedom to continue to talk about Melissa—a vital part of my grief recovery process.

Meet the Family

Our schedules did allow us the opportunity to see each other once in California in December, but that was the only time we could get together from the end of Festival Con Dios until early in 2003. For

Christmas, Adrienne flew home to South Africa and I went back to Indiana. I knew I needed to tell my family about Adrienne. I had let my mom know about her, but not how serious I was about Adrienne—partly because I was still trying to determine exactly how serious I was—and had asked her not to tell the rest of the family yet.

There hadn't been anyone else since Melissa, and I expected everyone would have strong reactions the first time they heard I cared for someone else. Another factor at work was my history with relationships. I didn't date just to date. I didn't want to play games with a woman and risk hurting her if I didn't think I could potentially have a serious relationship with her. Because of that, I knew that when my family members heard about Adrienne, they immediately would assume I was serious about her.

While excited about what was happening with Adrienne, I wasn't looking forward to telling my family about her. I had no clue how to do so. I weighed making a big announcement to everyone against telling small groups of family members at a time.

I chose the announcement.

"You know that girl from The Benjamin Gate?" I asked. Before anyone could answer, I added, "I really like her. We're dating."

Whew! Got that one out!

My brother-in-law—April's husband, Trent—said, "That's awesome, dude!" I think that was the only positive reaction. My family is extremely gracious and warm. But they were rather taken aback at learning I was dating someone. I was hoping that wouldn't be the case because I really needed support after experiencing guilt over falling in love again.

I understood why they were shocked. They hadn't heard me talk of a woman other than Melissa like that, and they knew we were probably already pretty serious about each other. Plus, Adrienne was the front for a Christian rock band, a stereotype that didn't fit the person they had imagined for me after Melissa. (They didn't know yet how soft-spoken and sweet Adrienne actually is, and when they did meet her, they fell in love with her.)

With my cell phone almost attached to my ear while I was in Indiana, my dad took note of how much I was talking to Adrienne while she was visiting her parents. He asked to speak with me one day and said he wanted me to make sure I wasn't making the decision to date her based solely on emotions. My dad asked if I would take a break from talking to her and spend time praying and seeking the Lord about what He desired for her and me.

I told my dad I would, and when I told Adrienne about my conversation with him, she agreed we should temporarily halt the calls and committed to pray for us.

We didn't talk for a week. I missed talking to her, but that was a good time of prayer that affirmed what I was feeling for Adrienne. I think that week also created time for my family to deal with the reality that there was someone after Melissa. They expected that eventually I would fall in love, have another relationship, and probably even marry again. I was still working through my feelings of guilt, and after my announcement they had to start their own process of dealing with "someone else." That week was important because it allowed me to walk through the process with my family in person rather than while we were apart.

On a lighter note, there was another benefit from our week without calling each other. A short while after Adrienne returned to the United States—about the time it takes, say, for the previous month's cell phone bill to arrive in the mail—we realized how expensive international calls were. I had to help pay her bill of more than $700.

With my family prepared to meet Adrienne, I made the 350-mile drive to pick her up at the Nashville airport when she returned from South Africa. We went on what we determined was our first official date—dinner at P. F. Chang's—and I brought her back to Lafayette to introduce her to my family.

Adrienne immediately won over everyone in my family. But I don't know who was more impressed with her—them or me. Seriously.

It's difficult enough meeting that special someone's parents for the first time. But it's exponentially more difficult when all around the family's house are photos of your special someone with his first wife.

Adrienne was amazing. I watched her not only interact with my family but also handle the Melissa situation, and I was like, *Now that is a special woman of God!*

She completely understood that it was a bit of a struggle for my family to see me with someone other than Melissa. Adrienne showed no hint of insecurity, and I can't imagine many people could go into that situation and not feel at least some uneasiness.

When we talked about the visit later, Adrienne told me, "I didn't go in there trying to replace Melissa or asking, 'Where's my place?' I wanted to go and support, not replace. I didn't want your family to feel like they had to get over Melissa. I wanted them to feel freedom to feel the emotions they were feeling."

Adrienne and my mom especially hit it off. During one of their trips to the grocery store, my mom shared at great length what we all had gone through with Melissa as a family, and how much Melissa had meant to all of us. My mom told me later that as she talked about Melissa, she could see a deep compassion in Adrienne's eyes. By the end of their conversation, they were crying with each other.

You would have thought Adrienne had been a part of our family for years. We all sat up late and talked, and there were some nights when the rest of us went to bed and left my mom and Adrienne talking at the kitchen table, where they would stay until three or four o'clock in the morning.

One time when I was alone with my parents, I let them know how serious I was about Adrienne. "She really is the one for me," I told them. That didn't go over too well. It was particularly hard for my mom to hear, and also for my sister when she found out what I had said. Their reservations had nothing to do with Adrienne but the fact that they were still working through their own grieving processes over Melissa.

They didn't let on to Adrienne about their feelings, and I think the way that she talked openly and with admiration about Melissa helped them more easily accept that Adrienne and I were headed down the relationship path.

Chapter 15

ALL ABOUT GOD

After Adrienne's visit with my parents, we went back on the road
with our respective bands. For me, that meant a new experience.

For Festival Con Dios, we had toured with a bunch of other musicians, and I had the good fortune of traveling by bus. It also was a
relatively short tour, to forty cities.

In 2003, though, the schedule included about 220 dates with 300
days on the road. And instead of a bus, we traveled by van with trailer
in tow. Part of the time, my band consisted of only me and drummer
Leif Skartland, and we opened for Bebo Norman. Leif, by the way,
started out with our band just before Festival Con Dios and still is
my drummer.

After touring with Bebo, we had a four-person band, and I bought
our first touring van—a Chevy Mark III that had a bed in the back
that we took turns sleeping in as we sometimes drove overnight to
get to the next show. I also performed concerts with Jars of Clay, and
I took part in the Ichthus festival in Kentucky that my family had
attended when I was young.

That first full year of touring was a good introduction to the not-
so-glamorous side of music. Once, we drove all the way from Southern

California to eastern Canada to play in a show—and the promoter never paid us.

It's a tough, tough business, and most people would be shocked to hear how many acts struggle to stay out of debt. Being a new artist, like I was, you feel the need to play just about anywhere to get your name out there, build up a following, and sell enough records to keep your label happy and interested in re-signing you when your contract expires.

I've joked that in my first full year out on the road, I played in small, dingy barns. I didn't, but I would have if a farmer had invited me and told me he had enough outlets to plug in all our extension cords.

I remember concerts with 30 to 50 people in the audience. It's no exaggeration to say I was stoked when I could look out before a concert and see 150 in attendance. One night, we actually had 600 people show up and I was crazy shocked.

During one of our trips, my wallet was stolen. The next time I was home in California, I went to the Department of Motor Vehicles office to get a new driver's license. I was hurriedly walking toward the entrance, talking to Adrienne on my cell phone, when a young guy who looked like he might be homeless came up to me and said, "Hey, man, you got some money?"

Not wanting to be slowed or distracted, I said, "No, sorry, man," and continued my conversation as I went into the DMV. Inside, as I waited to get my license replaced, I began to feel bad about how I had brushed off the guy and prayed, *Lord, give me an opportunity to see that guy again.*

After I finished at the DMV, I drove to a nearby In-N-Out Burger. Outside the restaurant, I saw the same guy. I couldn't believe it. I was so excited that God had given me another opportunity, and I wasn't going to miss this one.

I walked up to him and said, "Hey, man, come on inside, and I'll buy you some lunch."

After we ordered and sat down, I prayed for our meal and asked him to tell me his story.

His name was David, and he was, indeed, homeless. He said he was a heroin addict and an alcoholic. His wife had told him to leave their house, and he had been living underneath a bridge for a while. After telling me his story, he began asking questions about me.

One was what my job was.

"I play Christian music," I told him. He asked my name again.

"Jeremy," I answered.

"Not Camp?" he asked.

I nodded. I was surprised that he knew who I was.

David told me that before leaving his home, a friend had given him my first CD. As we ate, we talked about the Lord, my music, and our stories. When we were wrapping up, I felt strongly that I should really encourage David.

"God's going to restore your marriage," I told him. "I want you to be encouraged. He's brought me into your life at this moment for a reason."

We prayed, I gave David all the money I had in my wallet— twenty-six dollars—and gave him my cell phone number. I told him to call me if he needed anything and asked that he call me sometime to let me know how he was doing.

About eight years later I received an e-mail from a woman introducing herself as the wife of a drug-addicted homeless man I had met at an In-N-Out a long time before. She asked if I remembered the meeting, which I did. The woman said David was clean now and that they were back together. Then she said she e-mailed because she wanted to surprise her husband by arranging for him to see me again and asked if I could help make that happen.

I was all over that opportunity, and we arranged a meeting. It turned out that David's marriage had been completely restored by God, he and his wife were doing great, and they had a son whom I was also able to meet. It was an incredible reunion and made me so thankful that the Holy Spirit had granted me a second chance after I had brushed David off outside the DMV.

That's one of my favorite examples of the importance of finding some way to reach out when the Holy Spirit prompts us to help someone. We never know the fruits that can come out of our obedience. It also made me realize that if my wallet had not been stolen, I might not have met David. That gave me a new perspective on the importance of remembering when we go through frustrating times that God might be at work and how He can turn negative situations into testimonies for His glory.

Popping the Question

Adrienne and I needed to keep recharging our cell phone batteries because phone calls remained our primary mode of communication. On the rare days when one of us was free and in relatively close proximity to the other, we'd drive several hours to see each other.

Our relationship had a few ups and downs. They weren't any different from what most couples go through in a relationship, but we prayed together and on our own about them, and we worked our way through them by talking openly and honestly. Having those talks confirmed for both of us that we were serious about our relationship, and we came out of that time stronger in our love for each other.

Each spring the Gospel Music Association holds what is known as GMA Week. It basically is a huge annual conference for the gospel music industry, with just about anybody who's anybody in Christian music showing up. The GMA Dove Awards ceremony is the marquee event of the week.

Because I would be in Nashville for GMA Week, I was going to get to see Adrienne. And because I was going to get to see Adrienne, I took a nice ring along with me.

That was a very busy week for me because I did a lot of media interviews due to my being labeled an "up and coming" artist. There also were a number of activities for me related to promotion and marketing. Adrienne was busy, too, and we didn't get to see much of each other.

We had decided, though, that we definitely were going to get together for dinner one night during the week. But when?

The Benjamin Gate had been nominated for a Dove Award—for Modern Rock/Alternative Album of the Year—but Adrienne didn't expect her band would win. So I suggested we go out and eat *during* the Dove Awards. Then she asked if we could dress up for dinner anyway, even though we wouldn't be going to the Doves.

Dinner? Dressed up? Sounded to me like a good time to propose.

I made a reservation and a few arrangements at Park Cafe and picked up Adrienne. We were both exhausted from the hectic week, but on the way to the restaurant, it seemed like we took on an "exhausted peace" as we listened to worship music and talked over all the things that happened that week.

The restaurant had reserved a window table for us in an area with only one table nearby. It was a perfectly quiet place to catch up and, more important, for the top item on my dinner agenda.

I was trying to play it all cool, but I was nervous and probably acting a little giddy. We ordered our dinner and continued the conversation we had started in the car. I was so excited and having trouble hiding it.

I told Adrienne I needed to go to the restroom, but instead I took the engagement ring to a member of the restaurant staff for my big surprise coming later.

The food came, and we ate a delicious meal. Afterward, the waiter brought us small decorative boxes that looked like they could have had chocolates or some other treat in them. Adrienne's ring was inside her box. But she didn't open the box! We kept talking, and I kept waiting on her to reach for it. (Plus, I wanted to make sure the person I had handed the ring to hadn't studied the ring, decided to quit his job on the spot, and headed for a pawn shop.)

I had hidden a small CD player under the table, and as I wondered whether Adrienne was going to open her box, I reached under the table and started fidgeting with the player. Adrienne looked at me kind of funny, and I unsuccessfully tried to act like the commotion with my leg under the table was normal.

Finally, I just picked up the CD player so I could see the buttons and started playing the song "Here I Am to Worship." Adrienne had told me on several occasions that she wanted to walk down the aisle to that song.

With her song playing, I stood up, walked around to her side of the table, picked up her box, opened it, and pulled out the ring. I then dropped to a knee and asked, "Will you marry me?"

"Yes!" Adrienne said.

By that point the couple at the table near us had stopped their conversation to watch us. "Oh my goodness!" one of them said when I dropped to a knee, and after Adrienne accepted, they congratulated us.

We left the restaurant, and for at least the next thirty minutes, we both called our families and closest friends to deliver the news. And then to celebrate? Well, we went our separate ways again. I hit the road that night to resume touring, and it was about a month until the next time I saw my fiancée.

Breaking Up (But Not Us)

Our engagement signaled the official end of Adrienne's run with The Benjamin Gate. Back when Adrienne had returned to South Africa for Christmas, she was not happy with how things were going with the band, especially spiritually. She asked her family and friends at home to pray with her about the band's future.

That was a stressful time for Adrienne. She had not been an

original member of the band, so it had existed before without her, and the group's name wasn't "Adrienne Liesching and The Benjamin Gate," but in any band the lead singer carries the most prominent role. Adrienne was concerned that her leaving could end the musical careers of the other members, and she loved performing and being around the guys.

All of them were from South Africa, and The Benjamin Gate was pretty much everything they all had in the United States. Each of the guys in the band had sacrificed so much to leave his home country to try to make a go of it here together, and replacing the lead singer would require starting all over in many regards. Adrienne didn't think the other members would want to go through that process again.

When Adrienne came back to the States, she met with the other members of TBG to end the band. It was a difficult conversation for her to start, and understandably there was a bit of a negative reaction at first. But very shortly it became a mutual decision for the band to come to an end.

With the obvious direction our relationship was headed, the band members decided to wait until we had become engaged so that their breakup could become a positive "moving on," and Adrienne agreed to stay on for nine more months to play out the schedule so they wouldn't walk away in debt.

After we became engaged, it was announced that The Benjamin Gate would disband, and Adrienne and the guys continued to play into September.

Wedding Plans

Adrienne and I were able to see each other a few times, but not nearly enough for our preferences. Adrienne went to visit my family a couple of times without me, even going to Lafayette in July to celebrate her birthday with them. She would tell me how everyone had already made her a part of the family and how my parents were the most incredible Christians she had ever met. She admired their relationships with the Lord and picked their brains about how they maintained their close walk with Him after Melissa had gone to heaven.

Adrienne loved getting to know my mother's heart. They quickly grew especially close, and my mom became like a mentor to Adrienne. Imagine how cool it must have been for a mother to mentor the young woman her son was going to marry.

My dad would crack Adrienne up. He was fascinated with the differences between the United States and Adrienne's home country, except he kept getting South Africa and Australia mixed up.

At first when my dad asked questions about "Australia," Adrienne would give the best answer she could because she had an uncle who lived there. When she figured out that my dad actually intended to ask about South Africa, she started giving answers based on what her uncle had told about living in Australia, then sweetly say, "But in South Africa, where I live . . ."

We had set a December wedding date in South Africa, and Adrienne had booked a church and taken care of just about all the arrangements. But about three months before the wedding, Adrienne learned of potential complications with her visa because of the breakup of The Benjamin Gate and our pending marriage.

She was advised that if she were quizzed about her status while we were leaving South Africa, she could lie and return to the United States without problem. There was no way we were going to lie, though, so we had to move our wedding to the States.

Adrienne was able to quickly make all the changes for moving the wedding except for one thing. South Africa's seasons are the opposite of here, so the friend who made her dress made it for South Africa's warm weather. So Adrienne would have to get married in Indiana in December in a dress with very short sleeves. When Adrienne's time with The Benjamin Gate ended in September, she needed a place to stay, so she moved into my parents' house and lived in an extra bedroom. At least that gave her a chance to work on wedding details with my mom, so they were able to share that experience.

My parents cleaned out a place in the basement that would become her wedding headquarters. There she could work on decorations and the invitations. Adrienne hand made every invitation—somewhere between 150 and 200 of them. She began making them while she was still traveling with her band. When it wasn't her turn to drive, she sat in her seat and wrote out invitations. Preparing for the wedding and our future helped take her mind off the pending breakup of TBG.

One day after she had moved into my parents' home, my parents were looking through family pictures and came across some of me with Melissa. My dad got up from his seat, walked over to Adrienne, and gave her a big hug. "I just want you to know," he told her, "that we love Melissa. But she's with Jesus now and you're here, and we do see you as a part of the family."

My dad also told her, "God has selected you to be a tool to help heal my son. You're part of the healing plan for Jeremy."

Another time, right before the wedding, my mom talked to Adrienne about a wedding photo of Melissa and me that was displayed in the hutch in our family room. "I don't know why it is so hard for me to take that down right now, but I want you to know that I'll take it down before your family gets here."

Adrienne completely understood and told my mom there was no rush. Even telling the story now it sounds like that could have been an awkward moment, but it wasn't because of the way both my mom and Adrienne were sensitive to each other's feelings.

I didn't meet Adrienne's parents, Rory and Wendy, until they came to Indiana for the wedding, but there is an interesting story about me asking for her father's blessing to propose.

As a teenager, Adrienne had told her dad that if he didn't approve of the person she wanted to marry, she wouldn't marry him. Well, her dad had a serious struggle with the thought of giving the nod to someone he had never met even though he thought I sounded okay on the phone, liked what Adrienne had told him about me, and could see that she was happy with me. Still, without having talked with me in person, he wondered how he could give his approval of the marriage, until one day he sensed God telling him, "You don't have to—I already have."

When I placed "the call" to her dad, I was nervous and stammered around a little.

"Are you asking for my daughter's hand?" her dad asked.

"Yes," I answered.

"Even though I've never met you," he said, "and I always thought I'd meet all my kids' spouses before they'd marry, I see how Adrienne has grown and I see her joy when I hear her talk about you."

Whoa! I thought. *That's pretty rad!*

To make sure we got the timing right, we waited a little while after we became engaged to let Melissa's family know I was getting married again. Later, Adrienne mailed them an invitation.

Adrienne was thrilled to meet Melissa's two sisters, Megan and Heather, about a month before our wedding when she and my mom went to California to attend a retreat for pastors' wives.

Meeting Megan and Heather gave Adrienne the opportunity to express to them her admiration for Melissa and learn more about her from her sisters. Adrienne got along really well with them from the start, and they stayed in contact with one another. During one of their later conversations, Heather told Adrienne that following Melissa's death, she had grown closer to God; she felt comfort from the Lord stronger than she had ever experienced, and, as a result, her spiritual walk was deeper than ever before.

At the retreat for pastors' wives, Adrienne also met Jon Courson's second wife, Tammy. Of course, I had told Adrienne about Jon's importance to me, that he was the speaker when I had rededicated my life at summer camp and had encouraged me and Melissa's brother, Ryan, at his home after Melissa passed away. As a second spouse of a husband who had lost his first wife through tragedy, Tammy was able to encourage Adrienne with valuable wisdom.

Tammy told Adrienne, "There are certain places not to go in your mind, not comparing yourself." Then to prepare Adrienne for what might come up in our marriage, she gave Adrienne examples of how she had handled situations and memories regarding Jon's first wife.

Although I had consciously avoided making comparisons between Adrienne and Melissa, there still were times, naturally, when Adrienne made comparisons in her own mind. When that happened, she and I would talk through it, but it helped Adrienne immensely to hear Tammy's perspective on comparisons.

Because Tammy was the wife of a pastor who shared his testimony publicly, she also zeroed in on an area she knew would be vital for Adrienne to address before we married. Tammy asked a question that would have been difficult for me to answer if I had been Adrienne: "If Jeremy never shared about you from the stage, and only shared about Melissa, would you be okay with that?"

Adrienne answered that she would be because she had witnessed some of what God had done, not only through my testimony of walking by faith but also through the story I told of Melissa's life.

When Adrienne told me about her conversation with Tammy, she told me that question had been a good check in her heart to remind her that it wasn't about her, or even Melissa, but about the work that God was performing in countless people's lives.

And that was a good check for me as the one onstage sharing the stories and singing the songs from that season of my life. None of it was about me; it was *all* about God.

Chapter 16

REACHING
THE ROOTS

Adrienne and I married on December 15, 2003, in a small ceremony in Lafayette. Because my parents' church was meeting in a coffeehouse at the time, we married in an older church that had huge stained-glass windows.

At the start of the ceremony, when I was at the front of the church and gazing up the aisle for my first look at Adrienne in her wedding dress, my heart was pounding. Then when she took her place at the end of the aisle, I was blown away by how beautiful she was. I remember how big her smile was. I could tell she was just so happy, and that made me feel even happier than I already was. Adrienne was the perfect wife for me, a true gift from God and yet another sign of redemptive hope.

My dad was performing the ceremony, and I looked over to see him crying. I thought, *Oh my goodness, pull yourself together here. You've got to speak to the congregation in a minute.*

Instead of the traditional "Wedding March," "Here I Am to Worship" played as Adrienne walked down the aisle. Our friend

Jean-Luc led us and the congregation in a time of worship, and the Lord's presence was so strong in that church. That was *exactly* what we wanted because we wanted a ceremony with God's glory firmly on display to set the tone for the rest of our lives together. Adrienne's artistic flair also helped set that tone for the ceremony. As she had prayed about our wedding, the theme of *crowns* kept coming to her. During one time of prayer, the Lord placed Isaiah 35:10 on her heart: "And those the LORD has rescued will return. They will enter Zion with singing; everlasting joy will crown their heads. Gladness and joy will overtake them, and sorrow and sighing will flee away."

She took that as a promise for us from the Lord that all the sorrow would be removed from my life and that gladness and joy would overtake me and crown our heads.

Adrienne liked crowns and reflecting on God's royalty. On each of the invitations she attached a small wire crown she had made and wrote our promise verse from Isaiah under the crown. For the ceremony Adrienne made crowns for the flower girls and ring bearer to wear. From the invitations to the ceremony, we wanted it clear that Jesus would be King of our marriage.

It was an emotional ceremony, and tears flowed throughout. I cried, Adrienne cried, my dad cried at the front of the church. My dad cried big time, just as he had while officiating my first wedding.

We made a change from the traditional vows. We wrote our own vows and did not include "till death do us part" or "as long as we both shall live." Leaving out those two phrases had nothing to do with my commitment to Adrienne in our marriage. I was and am completely committed to her. But those phrases were difficult for me to think about—especially the first one. The word *death* seemed to leap out at me when I thought about reciting it during the ceremony. It struck a part of my emotions that remained tender. Adrienne was so understanding and supportive of that.

I wanted to be sensitive to Adrienne too. This was her first wedding, and I recognized that most brides grew up dreaming of their wedding day. Adrienne certainly had put a lot of planning and her creative talents into our wedding, and I wanted it to be Adrienne's big day. The radiant smile she displayed throughout the ceremony told me that it was.

My mom later said that what most stood out to her during the wedding was how radiant Adrienne appeared in her gown. My mom talked about how, while Adrienne was living with them during our engagement period, she had witnessed Adrienne changing from a shy, sweet girl into a confident, godly woman. During the wedding, the completion of that transformation struck my mom. Adrienne and I were so excited to be stepping from that church and into the next chapter of our lives. After the honeymoon, we sold the house I'd had in California in only a month, packed up everything, and moved to Lafayette so we could be near my family when we weren't on the road.

Heading into our marriage, we had talked about having kids. Three or four sounded like a good number to us. We both really loved kids and looked forward to starting a family. In fact, we were so excited about starting our own family that, well, let's just say it didn't take long.

We hadn't decided to have a baby right away, but if I can get away with using a double negative to describe our mind-set, we didn't try not to have a baby either.

About two months after we married, we learned that Adrienne was pregnant. It wasn't a major surprise to us, but it was for the people we told. I'm sure our announcement quickly made some math majors out of family and friends, calculating, *If they married in December and the baby is due in late September, let's see, that's one month, two months, three months . . .* Don't worry, everything was biblical!

In September 2004, Isabella Rose (Bella) was born. A year and a half later, Arianne Mae (Arie) joined the family. The girls were the most amazing blessings I could have imagined. Becoming a dad opened my eyes to a whole new perspective on life. Before they were old enough to crawl, and even before they were old enough to start moving around in their cribs, I watched in fascination as they began to discover the world around them.

Studying them made me want childlike eyes to view the world God had placed me in. One thing I enjoyed about having small kids was observing how uncomplicated life was to them. Life is so simple for young children. It's as we get older that we make life more involved and complicated and confusing than it needs to be. No wonder Jesus said this to a group of adults—His disciples—who were having a childish debate over which one of them would be the greatest in heaven: "Truly I tell you, unless you change and become like little children, you will never enter the kingdom of heaven."[13]

The births of Bella and Arie, however, also opened up a new set of fears for me. For a reason I can't explain, after Adrienne and I married, I had never felt any fear of her passing away. But when both girls were born, I experienced anxiety and wondered, *Would God possibly think of taking one of them home?* I was so terrified that one or both of them might die that I would hold them tight to me and pray extra hard for their protection.

That fear was very real. God had to persistently work on me in that area, as evidenced by the fact that a year and a half after having those fears with Bella, I experienced them again with Arie when she was born.

To the Foot of the Cross

One time when I was telling God how much I loved my girls and expressing how much I feared one of them passing away, God spoke to my heart gently but also with a don't-doubt-this firmness: *Do you not understand how much I love you, Jeremy? I love you perfectly, so much more than you ever could love your children.* I had been hoping that God would respond with something along the lines of "I love the girls, too, and everything's going to be just fine with them." But as I've learned with God through the years, He prefers to work below the surface of our problems. Although the fear of something bad happening to my daughters consumed my thoughts at times, the truth was that the fear was a surface issue, and God wanted to work on the root of my problem: I needed a better understanding of *His* love.

I didn't experience one of those instantaneous realizations, but God began walking me through a process of gaining better knowledge of the depth of His love. The Bible says that "God is love."[14] His very character, His essence, is love. Love is who He is. I struggled to grasp that truth because I was thinking in my limited, human terms.

Our love is conditional. No matter how much we would like to believe otherwise, we will always attach conditions to our love. We can say we will love someone no matter what, but that will change if we are slapped by rejection enough times from that person.

God's love is perfect. His love has no conditions. No circumstances can change it. Our Lord, our King, sees every ounce of our being and—if we are completely honest with ourselves—the grossness of who we are. And He still loves us! That love shone so greatly on the cross.

Our love can't be perfect, but God's love can't be anything but perfect.

We love, but God is love. There is an incredible difference between the two. I wish I could claim that I fully appreciate the difference. I don't, even though I'm still trying to comprehend it. I have learned, however, that one way to free myself from living in fear—such as the fear of experiencing death—is to increase my understanding of how much He loves and cares for me. The more I embrace the depth of my heavenly Father's perfect (unconditional) love for me, the easier it is for me to believe that all is well.

Just trust Me, God was telling me. *Trust Me. Trust Me. Trust Me.*

As I continued to pray that day, God reminded me of 1 John 4:18: "There is no fear in love. But perfect love drives out fear because fear has to do with punishment. The one who fears is not made perfect in love."

That verse soothed my spirit, and I repeated the words in my mind when I felt myself struggling with fear, regardless of what the fear was. Taking my focus off my circumstances to consider how much God loves and cares for me has washed away plenty of my fears.

Implied in that comment is that I still experience and wrestle with fear.

As I dealt with those early fears of one of my children passing away, I realized that I was afraid of the pain and heartache I had experienced with Melissa's passing. That was some of the worst pain I could imagine suffering, and I feared feeling that way again. Because I had come out on the other side of that experience, I knew that no matter what might happen to me, everything would eventually turn out fine. But I feared having to go through that pain again.

I wished there was a scripture I could flip to that would promise I would never have to go through that pain again. I've looked many times—sometimes desperately—and there is no such scripture. But what I can find in the Bible is, case after case, someone suffering and God walking with them every step of the way.

That's where God was, working on the *root* of my fear.

Gradually He brought me to a place where I could proclaim, "Lord, I believe that You will walk with me through whatever pain I will have to face in the future. By Your grace, I will not be afraid of the pain."

Peter addressed our being able to rejoice in God's sustaining power, "though now for a little while you may have had to suffer grief in all kinds of trials."[15]

Paul also offered insight on that subject in 2 Corinthians 4:16–18:

Therefore we do not lose heart. Though outwardly we are wasting away, yet inwardly we are being renewed day by day. For our light and momentary troubles are achieving for us an eternal glory that far outweighs them all. So we fix our eyes not on what is seen, but on what is unseen, since what is seen is temporary, but what is unseen is eternal.

Again, conquering fear and enduring suffering comes down to having and maintaining an eternal perspective. That's not an easy truth to hear during suffering because it certainly doesn't seem like our troubles are achieving anything at the time, but suffering is temporary.

I certainly didn't feel that way during my period of suffering, but I learned over time that it is true.

The suffering that God has walked through with me has refined me. It hasn't defined me; I'm not "the guy whose wife passed away and who has a powerful testimony because of that." But it has refined me and deepened my dependence on God.

Suffering digs to the very core of your soul and tests you, far below the shallowness of who you previously thought God was. Suffering asks, *Are you really going to trust the Lord? Are you really going to worship the Lord? Are you really going to still serve Him?*

"Yes" can be the only answer to those questions when you have been taken to a depth where you can understand and truly know who God is—to where you can experience personally who He says He is in the Bible—and then have to walk in that truth.

A friend suffered through the passing of his eighteen-year-old son. My friend told me, "Before this happened, I thought I had a strong relationship with God, but I was only in the meadow near the cross. After it happened, I went to the foot of the cross and stayed there."

As my friend and I learned through our experiences, suffering is an opportunity. Neither of us volunteered for our suffering. We had no option but to go through it. We did, however, have the option of how we responded. It was difficult, but we both chose to get up and walk to the foot of the cross.

Honestly, I don't believe I ever would have taken that journey if not forced to by my suffering. But trust me, once I made it to the foot of the cross, I knew I had never been closer to my Savior.

Chapter 17

ALL THAT TRULY MATTERS

The Lord continued to use my personal experiences to give me songs that resonated with people, who in turn amazed me with their stories of how the songs and my testimony had touched them and brought them encouragement and hope.

In the two years after Adrienne and I married, I saw tremendous growth musically. Six singles off my first CD reached number one, and I received four Dove Awards from the Gospel Music Association during that time. The success increased the platform from which I could share my message, thanks to more sales, more play time for my songs on radio stations, and more opportunities to headline tours.

Having an expanding ministry, however, required more from me. There was more touring, more people involved in the process, and more logistics to think about and manage.

Those expectations come with the territory in being part of Christian music, or any type of ministry for that matter. I was a preacher's kid, I attended Bible college, and I had good friends such as Jean-Luc in the Christian music industry, so I had an introductory knowledge of how time consuming my calling/career could become. I knew the demands could become a potential trap that Satan would love to see throw me off track from my duty to fulfill the Great Commission.[16] A good trapper will tell you a trap works best when it blends into the surroundings and his target doesn't know what it has stepped into until it's too late and the trap has sprung.

Fortunately I had a loving friend who boldly took a step to save me before I unknowingly walked into the trap.

I realized how busy I had become, but, hey, I thought that's just what came along with our band's success. Everything around me looked to be in good shape too. I was still seeking God and wanting to honor Him in everything I did. CDs were selling. The fact that we kept receiving story after story from fans indicated we were making the spiritual impact we wanted to make. At home, Adrienne and I were doing great. The kids were growing, and we were having wonderful times as a family.

But the pace was relentless. A growing ministry meant more work to be done so we could continue to grow and reach more people. We could hire people to do the work, so it wasn't like all the work was falling onto me. There was someone to arrange for the two buses and the two semis we took out on tour. There were people to unload the semis and set up all the equipment for each event. It wasn't like the van-and-trailer days when I was involved in the driving, the unloading, the performing, the reloading, and then the driving again.

So I wasn't necessarily doing more work in that regard, but I was responsible for more. My name had become a brand. (I have mixed emotions about that part of our industry, for sure.) The two buses and two semis that rolled into town, and all the people associated with the tour, were part of the Jeremy Camp show. If a crew member was rude to someone, guess what? He would go unnamed when the offended person would say, "That guy from Jeremy Camp sure was rude to me."

I was as prudent as possible in making hires, and I had great people working for me. But great people can make mistakes, and mistakes can happen that are beyond anyone's control. Things just seem to happen sometimes. The bigger we became, the more pieces we had, and having more pieces meant more opportunities for mistakes. Growth can create a vicious cycle.

But the bottom line was that if something was to go wrong, it would be on me—it would be on my name.

That load weighed heavily enough on my shoulders that I started trying to stay out ahead of any problems that might come up. When we did have problems—and I emphasize "we" because we did have people whose jobs were to take care of those problems—*I* tried to figure out how to solve them. Then I would get involved with how many shows we were planning, or how CD sales were going, or how frequently songs were being played on radio stations.

That's not to say that those things weren't important and I should have sat back and turned everything over to those working with me. I'm not a lazy person. But I was going too far in the opposite direction, taking on too much, and putting myself in places where, frankly, I didn't belong.

That overload is what made things become too time consuming for my own good. (And, perhaps, the good of those working with me.)

Those who have been through seasons when you were involved in more areas than you had time for probably are sitting there thinking, *Uh-huh, I see where this is headed.*

The Trap

When I was giving my time to situations where I didn't need to be, my personal time with the Lord suffered. I still spent time in His Word and prayed, and I still wanted to have an effective ministry and be a strong witness for Him. But my time with Him was inconsistent. In effect, I was spending less time with Him so I could do more things for Him. That is a potentially deadly trap. For example, I noticed that growth of the ministry brought more decisions that needed to be made quickly. When in the past I would have gone off by myself, gotten on my face on the floor, and prayed about the decision, I now was having to rush into decisions. *Snap! No time to go pray first*, I wrongly thought. I found in my business dealings that rarely were quick decisions good ones.

I was taking too much control. Although I'm not sure now how in control I actually was. A false sense of control is more like it.

I had allowed myself to become too busy trying what I thought was the best way to do the Lord's work. I had failed to put the Lord above the work. As a result, I began to feel burned out. I wanted out of the grind. When I wasn't on the road, I was recording. When I wasn't making a record, I was writing songs for the next one. If I wasn't doing that, I was doing interviews to promote a record or a tour. So many different things were pulling me in so many different directions. *I can't do anything else*, I thought.

Now I do want to make clear that there wasn't anything phony going on with our ministry because I've always done the best that I can to make sure everyone on our team has integrity that guides our decisions. Instead, I'd say our ministry had become misguided because I was trying to guide it more than I was allowing God to guide. We weren't going out on the road and taking people's money in exchange for merely putting on a good show for them. Every "performer" will have nights when he or she doesn't feel as good as normal because of a cold, a headache, allergies, a sore throat, a bad day at the office, and so on. So I'm not saying I didn't experience those nights. But even when I was burning out, I took very seriously the ministry aspect of every event. My purpose remained unchanged: to glorify God. And He continued to work through our events despite the limitations I was putting on Him on the business side.

In fact, I would say because glorifying God remained our purpose, that goal added to the burden I was causing myself to carry. People's spiritual lives were at stake, and I got that. The livelihoods of those who traveled with us were at stake. As Jeremy Camp, I needed to be pouring into everyone who was on the road. But I was tired and burning out, so I didn't have much to give. Because I didn't feel encouraged myself, I had a hard time encouraging them.

I wanted out of music, at least the way I was doing it. I started weighing whether I should leave the music industry and become a worship leader in a church. Or perhaps a youth pastor.

Uncertain of where I was headed, I operated with a sense of uneasiness. That uneasiness, I soon learned, was my spiritual "check engine" light, and I was ignoring it because I was too busy to stop and get my engine checked.

One day, a pastor friend for whom I had a tremendous amount of respect pulled me aside and asked, "Jeremy, who's steering this ship—is it the Lord, or is it you?"

His question hit me right between the eyes!

I've been blessed to have various people in my life who would speak the truth in love to me, so I was accustomed to that type of question. But I couldn't think of anyone who had been that direct with me concerning my career. I didn't get defensive with my friend because I appreciate a trusted advisor bold enough to be that blunt with me.

But his question broke me.

I didn't have to evaluate for long to recognize that I had been steering the ship. I had been trying to set the direction as everything became bigger and better, working night and day trying to control the outcomes.

I had been asking the Lord what He wanted me to do next, where He wanted the ministry to go. I aimed to be excellent in all that we did so that He would be glorified. But what I had stopped doing was waiting on the Lord to lead and to confirm before I moved ahead. I wasn't being willfully disobedient, but I was taking control and getting out ahead of God.

My dad used to say, "We can get so busy doing the work of the Lord that we forget the Lord of the work." That was me.

I found myself recalling how things were growing up. There were times when our family had nothing, yet following what our parents modeled for us helped us be content. Then I would contrast those memories with how discontented I had become as the result of having so much. I mean, I was successful. The Lord had propelled me into the music industry so purely, with gratitude, joy, and humility. I still felt grateful, but honestly, I had reached a point for the first time in my life where I thought (wrongly) that I didn't need the Lord to guide me.

I'm ashamed to admit that, although I wouldn't go so far as to speak these words, the attitude behind my prayers had become "Thanks, God, but I've got it from here."

As a result, the joy had waned. The enemy who comes to "steal and kill and destroy" had set a nicely covered trap for me.[17] I was serving the Lord, and there was no doubt that He was in what we were doing; visible results backed up that belief. But the success—the sales, the number-one songs, the awards—were the ground cover disguising the trap I was headed directly toward until one person loved me enough to confront me with a question that changed my course for the better.

Relinquishing the Wheel

Through my friend's simple but pointed question, the Holy Spirit convicted me about needing to step away from the ship's wheel.

I dedicated myself to studying the Bible more and refocusing on Scripture. I committed to more time of serious prayer, and I'm talking face-on-the-floor type of prayer time. I also sought out leaders and friends whom I knew could and would give me godly counsel—even when I didn't specifically ask for it.

As a band, we had continued to study the Bible together and pray before we went onstage, but those times had become more of a routine than they needed to be. We committed to really digging into the Word again during our Bible studies.

All the above led to a deeper sense of the Lord's presence in my life. When we are more deeply aware of God's presence, we become more aware of additional ways through which He can speak to us. One of those ways led to a key monumental breakthrough moment in my life.

I was doing a media interview, sharing Melissa's story and my testimony. I retold the conversation when she had said if one person were to come to know Christ because of her cancer, it would be worth all her suffering. As soon as I said that, it struck me how many people I knew of—and I knew there had to be many more in addition to those—who had accepted Jesus as their Savior or gone deeper in their relationship with Him because of Melissa's inspiration.

I don't remember the rest of the interview, but I remember hanging up the phone afterward and feeling like a dam had just broken. I couldn't have stopped crying if I had wanted to.

It was like the Holy Spirit was telling me, *Remember why you started doing this. Remember what it's for. Remember "the one person."* "Lord," I prayed, "I want my focus to stay on You. I want You to be my first love again. I want to be led by You into the next season. You are in control, not me!"

I hadn't experienced a breaking like that since the day I drove down the mountain following my three days in the cabin. The Lord broke me big-time, and it felt great. Later that day, I wrote the song "Beyond Measure" as an expression of my desire to submit to the leading and lordship of Jesus in every aspect of my life—as a man, a husband, a father, and an artist.

(Verse 1)
The fog has finally cleared to see the beautiful life You've given
     me
To feel the breeze of my newborn's gentle breath
With one to walk hand in hand
To share this life that You have planned
It's like a storybook with dreams
That are meant to see every next step is an extraordinary scene

[Chorus]
I know that I've been given more than beyond measure
I come alive when I see beyond my fears
I know that I've been given more than earthly treasure
I come alive when I've broken down and given You control

(Verse 2)
I've faced a great tragedy but have seen the works of what You
     bring
A display of faith that You give
I don't know if I will ever understand
The depth of what it is You've done inside
But I know that I won't find any worth apart from You

[Bridge]
Everything that I have has been given so unselfishly
And shown that even when I don't deserve
You always show the fullness of Your love[18]

The first line of the chorus—"I know that I've been given more than beyond measure"—represented my renewed appreciation for God's good gifts. I had been blessed more than beyond measure. I had been blessed to travel to sing songs, lead worship, and witness the

Lord touching lives through our ministry. I was blessed to come home to a beautiful wife and an awesome little girl (this was BA—Before Arie), and to see my family's needs being met. I didn't get into music ministry to make a lot of money, and my purpose hadn't changed even with success. The Lord, though, had started to provide some of those added blessings.

The final line of the chorus summarized where I was at that point in my life: "I come alive when I've broken down and given You control."

The peripheral things—the number of shows, the sales, the radio time—had become too important to me, and I was coming back to an important realization: *All that truly matters is God.*

I just needed to give up on the idea that I was in control.

We want control, but God wants our hearts. His Word makes that clear. Just two examples:

Luke 10:27: "He [Jesus] answered, 'Love the Lord your God with all your heart and with all your soul and with all your strength and with all your mind.'"

Matthew 6:33: "But seek first his kingdom and his righteousness, and all these things will be given to you as well."

I'd had plenty of experience with having God as my all. He was all my family had when my parents had limited income and we needed groceries. He was all I had at Maranatha Christian School when I covered my tuition with a scrub brush and a vacuum cleaner. He was all I had in California when I lived with my friend's grandma Marge, depended on friends for rides, and borrowed guitars to play in churches. He was all I had in the darkest moments after Melissa had gone to her eternal home.

Now that I had reached a level of success through which I could be self-sufficient, God still wanted to be my all.

When I had finally been forced to admit that I was steering the ship and then decided to turn the wheel back over to Him, He reminded me: "I want you to love Me and rest in My love for you. I'll take care of everything else. I'm in control anyway, not you. Your illusion of power is just that—an illusion—and it needs to be broken down."

What a relief!

Chapter 18

THERE WILL BE A DAY

With my priorities realigned, God continued to pour out His blessings and prove His faithfulness to me every day.

Arie entered our world in 2006. I thought all my heart had been melted when our first daughter, Bella, had been born, but Arie somehow found a whole new chunk of heart to melt!

I've been asked how having children affected my music. I'm sure those who ask are hoping for—perhaps even expecting—a profound answer. I usually disappoint them because even today I can't look back and see a direct impact musically (although being a father certainly has provided me more humorous stories to tell during shows).

Having two kids, however, did give me a much deeper understanding of my heavenly Father's heart. As Bella and Arie began to grow and become more active, they became crawling and then walking reminders of God's grace and love. As a father, I learned more about my Father.

Our music ministry was continuing to be blessed too. I was grateful that BEC offered me a second contract, and I gladly signed it. I also had the distinct honor and privilege to be coproducer of the debut solo album of my favorite person in the world: Adie Camp.

As I continued to tour, I kept on sharing Melissa's story and my journey to becoming able to walk by faith. And I noticed a funny thing: the publicity came in waves. After I first came onto the music scene and had some well-known songs and won a couple of awards, I was asked a lot about my story for interviews in the Christian music circles. So there were a lot of people I met or received e-mails from who wanted to talk about my story. For the most part, my story was nearly all anyone wanted to talk about. Then I went through that time of (unsuccessfully) trying to steer the ship.

When I emerged from that season without having sunk the ship before I handed over the wheel to God, another wave of attention followed. Much of it came in interviews with secular media and bigger Christian media outlets with a more general audience than music specific. All of a sudden, I began hearing from fans who said they had never heard my story.

Allow me to say this about number-one songs and awards: they are not my ultimate goal at all. My ultimate goal is that God be glorified through my music.

That said, there are two perspectives to take on writing well-known songs and winning awards.

First, from a purely musical standpoint, they are nice to receive. Even though they're not my ultimate goal, I've yet to hand one back! I'm a musician. We are creative people in a subjective business, and our work is both praised and criticized—sometimes at the same time. I have been given a gift from God. The lack of guitar training I had when I started out is proof of that. I have a gift, and it is my responsibility to do the best I can with that gift He gave me.

Being in a subjective business, I would be foolish to get caught up in all the awards and the numbers. But if fans are buying my CDs, downloading my songs, calling radio stations to request my songs, and voting for me to win awards, it would be insincere of me to say none of that is important. It is important, and I am grateful for the support.

The second perspective is that well-known songs and awards lead to a larger platform. God has placed songs on my heart and given me a testimony for a purpose: to share them with others who need hope and encouragement. Why wouldn't I want to do what is necessary to be able to share them with more people?

But, still, there was a point when I wondered if the time had come to stop sharing the story of Melissa and me.

I've used the word *story* a lot to describe what I share onstage. Really, though, *story* is a rather weak description. What I was sharing was a significant part of my life—and a painful one. God had worked a tremendous healing in me that even made it possible for me to get up on a stage and tell my story without completely breaking down. But there were still tender spots that would get poked and prodded as I shared. The pain was never going to go away. I didn't expect that. And I didn't want it to go away. That might sound odd, but I didn't want to ever tell the story without feeling pain. I didn't want it to ever become just a story.

Also, I wanted to be sensitive to Adrienne. From day one, she had been a tremendous support. When I would tell Adrienne that I was wondering if I should at least temporarily omit the story from performances, she would quickly encourage me to continue sharing—often by repeating Melissa's words: "If one person . . ." Adrienne would say she still loved to hear me share about Melissa's heart and her desire to be completely sold out to the Lord.

"God has used Melissa to touch my heart and so many other hearts, and that's part of who you are," Adrienne once told me. "Don't think for a minute that I am going to get in the way of this. I know how it ministers to people. I've seen the impact. This is too important."

Adrienne is an incredible wife, and as she so often does, she really nailed it on the head when she said, "This is too important." One night on the bus as I was praying specifically about whether I should continue telling Melissa's story, the Lord led me to a great passage that says God "comforts us in all our tribulation, that we may be able to comfort those who are in any trouble, with the comfort with which we ourselves are comforted by God."[19]

I had gone through tribulation and received God's comfort. Because of that, I had been placed in a position to lead others experiencing their own tribulations to the same comfort.

Melissa saw the one—the nurse—she had hoped and prayed would come to Christ through her cancer. I've had the blessing of seeing and hearing from the thousands more.

So I continue to share the story because I know so many hurting people need hope and encouragement as they deal with the suffering or passing of a loved one. I was one of them. Some days I still am.

Frankly, there is nothing on this earth I would choose to place my hope in. I've tried, and I've talked to many others who have done so too. We are all in agreement—placing hope in anything of this world does not work.

I've been through difficult times that left me hopeless, and I would rather not experience them again. Hopeless people want to give up because the suffering and the pain become too much to bear.

The conversations with those people at merch tables after concerts and the e-mails and letters they've sent me are so numerous that I would not even want to try to estimate their number. "Jeremy, your songs bring me hope and encouragement," they would tell me. While that was nice to hear, the truth was that their hope and encouragement was coming from the Lord. My songs were nothing more than the tools through which He had chosen to touch their hearts.

Looking Forward to Home

In more than ten years of touring, I've stayed in my fair share of hotels. I've stayed in a wide variety of hotels too. Some were so bad I wouldn't even want to drive by them again. Some spoiled me with their amenities and first-class service. Regardless of the place, do you know what my favorite thing to do at hotels is? Check out! Especially if I'm checking out to head home.

I can stay in a hotel where a bellhop carries my luggage to my room for me, room service brings a nice meal to me, and a maid makes my bed and cleans my room for me. But I still can't wait to leave that behind so that I can drive up to my house, carry my own suitcases inside to where my family is waiting to greet me, cook up some plain old burgers on the grill myself, and then perhaps even—harkening back to that one year of high school—vacuum the floor and scrub the commodes.

Why? Because that hotel may be nice, but it is *not* my home.

It is nothing more than a temporary place to stay.

We tend to lose sight of this reality that earth is not our true home; it's just a temporary place to stay. Heaven is my home, and I can't wait to check out of this old earth and head there. I think back to my friend Jean-Luc's words at Melissa's graveside: "Let's hasten the day!" In the midst of our trials and pain and suffering, we need to be heaven-minded.

My hope and your hope—*our* hope—is in heaven!

From experience, I can tell you that Revelation 21:4 offers great comfort to those in pain. It tells us that no matter how difficult our circumstances become, there will be a day that is worth hoping for: "'He will wipe every tear from their eyes. There will be no more death' or mourning or crying or pain, for the old order of things has passed away."

In Romans 8:18, Paul brought eternal perspective to difficulties when he wrote, "I consider that our present sufferings are not worth comparing with the glory that will be revealed in us."

Let me tell you, I've hurt. I've hurt to the point where I thought it couldn't get any worse, and then it did. I've hurt more than I ever thought I could hurt and survived. But as far as the pendulum has swung to the side of pain in my life, God's Word promises that there will be a day when the pendulum will swing even farther on the side of glory.

My hope is in those promises of glory!

Inspired by those verses in Revelation and Romans, I wrote the song "There Will Be a Day." When we recorded the song, we brought in a choir to sing the chorus and the bridge. A woman in the choir had been suffering from chronic pain. As she sang of the day with no more suffering and pain, she closed her eyes and raised her hands in worship, embracing the hope that someday she would be home, where she would no longer have to suffer through the pain she was experiencing on this earth.

That's a hope worth holding on to, and as one who has clutched it with all my might, it is a hope worth sharing because I know that "There Will Be a Day":

(Verse 1)
I try to hold on to this world
With everything I have
But I feel the weight of what it brings
And the hurt that tries to grab
The many trials that seem to never end
His word declares this truth
That we will enter in this rest
With wonders anew

[Chorus]
But I hold on to this hope
And the promise that He brings

That there will be a place with no more suffering
There will be a day with no more tears
No more pain and no more fears
There will be a day
When the burdens of this place
Will be no more
We'll see Jesus face-to-face

But until that day
We'll hold onto You always

(Verse 2)
I know the journey seems so long
You feel you're walking on your own
But there has never been a step
Where you've walked out all alone

Troubled soul, don't lose your heart
'Cause joy and peace He brings
And the beauty that's in store
Outweighs the hurt of life's sting.

[Chorus]
But I hold on to this hope
And the promise that He brings
That there will be a place with no more suffering
There will be a day with no more tears
No more pain and no more fears
There will be a day
When the burdens of this place
Will be no more
We'll see Jesus face-to-face

But until that day
We'll hold onto You always

[Bridge]
I can't wait until that day
When the very one I've lived for always
Will wipe away the sorrow that I've faced

To touch the scars that rescued me
From a life of shame and misery
This is why, this is why I sing

[Chorus]
There will be a day with no more tears
No more pain and no more fears
There will be a day
When the burdens of this place
Will be no more
We'll see Jesus face-to-face

There will be a day with no more tears
No more pain and no more fears
There will be a day
When the burdens of this place
Will be no more
We'll see Jesus face-to-face

There will be a day
He'll wipe away the tears
He'll wipe away the tears
He'll wipe away the tears
There will be a day[20]

Overwhelmed with Love and Peace

Late in the spring of 2009, we learned that Adrienne was pregnant with our third child. In August, when she went in for her fourteen-week checkup, the doctor could not find the baby's heartbeat. The doctor said that was not too unusual at that stage of a pregnancy. When Adrienne had an immediate follow-up ultrasound, the doctor said the baby's heart had stopped beating a week earlier.

We hadn't taken anything for granted with the pregnancy, but when Adrienne had entered into the second trimester, we had released an exhale at knowing the chances of a miscarriage drop at that stage. We were blindsided by the doctor's report.

Many times, I had observed Adrienne placing a hand on her growing belly and praying for the little one inside her. We had talked about our plans for preparing a baby room in the house and were looking forward to finding out whether we would have a third daughter or our first son. Bella and Arie were excited about having a new brother or sister.

We needed a strong sense of the presence of God, and as always, He was there for us. When Adrienne wrote about the miscarriage on our blog, she said, "God has overwhelmed us with His love and peace. We know He is faithful and don't doubt for a minute that He is in control. We are so thankful for the hope we have in Christ."

The day before we learned about the miscarriage, Adrienne had received a call from a friend with a prayer request about a local pastor's son who had been in a car wreck and was on life support. (The son later went to be with Jesus.) As their discussion continued, Adrienne's friend said she hoped the Lord would never test her faith in that way.

Adrienne thought about that conversation—particularly that last part—the rest of the day. The next morning in her prayer time, she got on her knees and told the Lord that she would never want to put limitations on what He could do in her life and that whatever He wanted her to walk through, she would gladly go through for Him.

Later that morning, the doctor said we had lost our baby.

When we informed my parents of the miscarriage, Adrienne told my mom about what she had prayed that morning. "Adrienne," my mom said, "the Lord is strengthening your testimony."

The morning after the ultrasound, we read Scripture together and focused on all the things that God had done in our lives and all that He was doing at the time. Psalm 16 was written at a time when David's life apparently was in danger. In the first verse, David declared that he would take refuge in God. In the remaining verses, in the face of the unsettling circumstances surrounding him, David confidently spoke of the trust he had in God. That was an especially comforting passage for us to share.

And, as usual, my mom was correct. Adrienne's testimony has been strengthened. With Twitter and blogs and the like, we had been publicly excited about the pregnancy. Our time of sorrow became equally public. But just as the Lord had done with me concerning Melissa, He turned difficulties into opportunities. Adrienne has been able to reach out to other women who have suffered through a miscarriage and tell them of the Lord's goodness in all circumstances.

Adrienne would later say that she came away from that painful trial with deeper insights on my loss of Melissa. Adrienne previously had felt sympathy for me. She would say things along the lines of, "Wow, I can't imagine going through that." She did not try to compare the miscarriage to Melissa's passing, but she did grieve losing a child we loved. As we grieved together, she told me, "I can empathize with you more and really understand some of what you felt."

The miscarriage of our baby made us appreciate even more having two healthy daughters to brighten our every day, but the miscarriage also touched on some of the fears I had previously had about one of our daughters passing away.

Maybe we're supposed to have two kids—that's why we had the miscarriage, I reasoned. I battled for a while with whether I wanted us to try to have another baby. I didn't want to go through anything like the miscarriage again. I didn't want to risk having to go through heartache again.

The biggest hurdle I faced was allowing myself to be vulnerable enough to trust God again.

After a while, though, I developed a real peace about trying to have another baby, knowing that no matter what might happen, God had a plan for our family and knew exactly what He was doing.

Late in 2010, we found out Adrienne was pregnant. We were excited, and although more cautious about the timing of when we made the news public, we had a complete trust in God for the welfare of our baby.

Because we had two girls, I got the "Do you want a boy or a girl?" question a lot. I was cool with having another girl because Bella and Arie were so sweet and so much fun. But when the doctor told us that the next one would be a boy, I was beaming. "He's going to be working out and playing football!" I said.

On August 17, 2011, our little rookie made his debut. We named him Egan Thomas. Egan means "zeal for the house of the Lord" and "young warrior." My mind-set toward Egan since his birth has been "Make him a warrior for You, Lord! May he never look to the right or the left, but keep his eyes on You!"

I've noticed something different about having a son after having two daughters. I want to be a man of God for my daughters, but with Egan I want to be an example of a man of God for him to follow. I realize that he will be watching my lead and how I relate to the Lord. I want him to see his dad as being passionate and sold out for Christ, as being uncompromising in his faith. And then I pray that this is the type of man Egan will become.

Chapter 19

RISKING IT ALL
FOR THE GOSPEL

I've always tried to be a good steward of the story God has given me. That He is still writing through me. Being a good steward includes trusting and following His timing.

Part of the strong interest my story has long attracted were numerous requests to turn my story into a book or a movie. I shared my story during concerts, but I didn't believe the story was complete enough to put into one of those formats. God was still walking me through the healing and the restoration and the new beginnings with Adrienne and our children.

While Adrienne was pregnant with Egan, I began to sense the time had come to take the next step with my story. In 2011, I released the first version of this book. The following year, I began work on a revised and expanded version with a different publishing strategy that would make my story available to more people. The book came out more than a decade after Melissa had gone to heaven, but I underestimated the difficulty of reliving that part of my life during the process of writing my story. *Reliving* is an accurate description.

In talking about my story with the people who helped make the book a reality, not only was I asked to recount details I had not thought about for so long, but I also needed to describe scenes I had tried to forget. That brought back a rush of pain and sadness I'd had to deal with.

In the aftermath of the book being published and hearing from people who read my story, I realized the level at which I was connecting with people was in direct relation to the depth I was willing to go in the writing process. I learned a valuable lesson about the power of our testimonies: although the circumstances of people's stories can vary greatly, the deeper we allow ourselves to plunge into our feelings and emotions with others, the more common ground we discover. There we can relate to one another, minister to one another, and experience God's healing together at deeper levels. In other words, I wouldn't find an enormous number of people whose spouses had cancer and who went to be with Jesus three and a half months after their weddings. My story consists of specific circumstances that perhaps few have experienced and been forced to overcome. But by digging into those issues of fear and trust I battled following Melissa's death, I connect with people who can relate to those issues regardless of the circumstances of their stories and, I pray, help them find what I had to accept in my life as a new normal.

Writing the earlier versions of this book was not an easy process, but it proved worthwhile. The desire to be a good steward of what God had done in my life continued after writing the book. Soon after its release, my manager, Matt Balm, received a call from Kevin Downes, who is an actor, writer, producer, and director active in the Christian film industry.

Kevin had recently played the role of Shane, one of the main characters, in *Courageous*. Faith-based films were seeing a surge in popularity at the time, and Kevin wanted to make a movie based on my book. We took the initial steps of finding a director and a writer to begin a script, but nothing we worked on felt right. I didn't want to force matters because outside of God's timing, a movie would not have been as effective as it could be. We put everything on hold, and I kind of forgot about it all.

Meanwhile, as the movie was not coming together, I heard from my youth pastor in Indiana, Jed Gourley. Jed, his sister-in-law Melanie, and her husband, Paul, were serving as missionaries in Kyrgyzstan, a 90-percent-Muslim country on the western border of China. Adrienne and I had started Speaking Louder Ministries in 2012, with a goal of bringing the message of Christ to every corner of the world. As part of our ministry, we partnered with churches in foreign countries to hold outreaches, including leadership and worship conferences, health-related help projects, and crusade-style events.

Jed e-mailed to ask if I would consider bringing my band to Kyrgyzstan. I researched Kyrgyzstan and learned the country was experiencing civil unrest and there was a crackdown on Christianity, with missionaries being removed from the country. I replied that considering the issues in Kyrgyzstan, a trip there didn't feel right to me.

Jed graciously responded, saying that if I didn't believe God wanted us to come to his country, he completely understood my reluctance. Then he added this might be the last such opportunity in his country because the government was shutting the doors on outreach and any bold declarations of Christianity. Churches were having to go underground.

Oh my goodness, I thought when I read those words. I knew Jed well and knew he wasn't trying to pressure me. I sensed a desperation in the tone of his e-mail. I began wondering how I could *not* go to Kyrgyzstan. I'd always talked about being completely sold out to God, and considering my story, I obviously had been through a lot in life. Through it all, God had shown Himself faithful. My latest album at the time was *Reckless*. The title song was about recklessly following where God leads.

Adrienne and I began praying. I informed the guys in the band of the request, and they prayed. We all ultimately felt a peace about going to Kyrgyzstan, and Jed started the process of having us cleared to come to his country.

The Kyrgyzstan Ministry of Religion and the State Committee for National Security (KGB) screened us online. Apparently, the awards they read about me receiving boosted our cause. They wanted to read the lyrics of our songs. Knowing how my lyrics talk about Jesus, I was like, *Dudes, check them out all you want!* We received approval to go, but they told us we could only perform our music and not share anything about our Christianity.

We monitored the news out of Kyrgyzstan, and I don't know if this was because of our increased awareness or this actually was the case, but the anti-Christian efforts there seemed to be intensifying. All of us still felt peaceful about going, but we also anticipated the trip would be interesting.

Watching My Back—And My Words

We scheduled a weeklong outreach of events and concerts in Kiev, Ukraine, en route to Kyrgyzstan. A thousand people showed up at one of our Kiev concerts, and hundreds of people gave their lives to Christ. After witnessing that incredible response, we boarded our plane for Kyrgyzstan on a high. Even though I had lost my voice after playing shows back-to-back, God clearly was orchestrating this trip.

We didn't know this at the time, but the day of our arrival in the capital city of Bishkek, CBN News published an article online titled "Secret Believers Share Faith Under Fire." The article described how believers from Kyrgyzstan and three neighboring countries were having to meet in secret in Kyrgyzstan because of increasing restrictions on religion and threats of Christians being beaten, arrested, or killed.[21]

When we touched down in Kyrgyzstan, a completely different feeling overcame us. As we stepped off the plane, the oppression was so heavy it felt like we were walking into a dark room with no idea of what was in the room and what would happen next. It felt like my chest was being pressed in. Everyone in our traveling group, which included my dad, had this weird feeling of *What's going on here?* At our hotel I felt a palpable resistance to what we were there to do: proclaim Christ. The next morning our group gathered and talked about the obvious need to pray. Through our prayer time we again began to feel peace flood over us about our decision to come to Kyrgyzstan and sensed an assurance that God would guide and protect us throughout our week there.

My dad spoke to a group of local churches, citing examples from his life of how our suffering magnifies the beauty and glory of God. My dad read from Philippians 1:12–14:

> Now I want you to know, brothers and sisters, that what has happened to me has actually served to advance the gospel. As a result, it has become clear throughout the whole palace guard and to everyone else that I am in chains for Christ. And because of my chains, most of the brothers and sisters have become confident in the Lord and dare all the more to proclaim the gospel without fear.

My dad's participation in the outreach was especially powerful in a culture that held high respect for parents and elders. And as we learned more about the fear of possible persecution under which local church leaders lived, that passage he read proved timelier and timelier.

During one prayer meeting, I read a portion of Scripture that Adrienne had e-mailed to me:

> His word is in my heart like a fire,
>> a fire shut up in my bones.
> I am weary of holding it in;
>> indeed, I cannot.
> I hear many whispering,
>> "Terror on every side!
>> Denounce him! Let's denounce him!" . . .
>
> But the LORD is with me like a mighty warrior;
>> so my persecutors will stumble and not prevail.
> They will fail and be thoroughly disgraced;
>> their dishonor will never be forgotten.
>
> Sing to the LORD!
>> Give praise to the LORD!
> He rescues the life of the needy
>> from the hands of the wicked. (Jeremiah 20:9–11, 13)

Both from within Kyrgyzstan and back home, we were receiving confirmation that the Lord would protect us.

My first big event for the outreach was a news conference. Of course, Ministry of Religion officials were there—they didn't try to hide their presence, either—to keep tabs on us and, specifically, what I said. American musicians visiting their country was a big deal, and my face was all over Bishkek on promotional materials. The anticipation of our arrival had been heightened by members of local churches translating our songs into Russian for not only the people of Kyrgyzstan but also the neighboring countries. The local news agencies wanted to hear why we had come to Kyrgyzstan. In fact, I was asked that question in a variety of ways during the news conference. Each time, I answered that we had come to perform our music for their country and their people.

One member of the press kept her eyes locked on me. She asked with a touch of forcefulness, "But *why* are you here?"

I would have loved to answer, "I want to tell people about Jesus and invite them to come forward to receive Him as their Lord and Savior." But I knew I had to be careful about what I said, especially regarding the name of Jesus.

"I've been through a lot in my life," I said and then offered an overview of my story. "God has given me a lot of healing," I concluded. "He has showed Himself faithful, and He's given me hope in the midst of adversity. I want to share that there is hope because we all go through hard times and struggles."

I couldn't tell if that answer satisfied the questioner, but she did loosen her stare.

I conducted more interviews after that news conference, and I felt a little bolder with each one. In one interview, I gave more of my testimony and talked about how Jesus saved my life.

Our outreach included a night of worship for youth from local churches. The youth were at the center of a major spiritual battle in Kyrgyzstan, with non-Christian philosophies pulling at them, not to mention high rates of drug and alcohol use. As I was walking into the venue, I overheard Jed telling someone, "We'll just have to deal with that later."

I stopped and turned toward Jed.

"Deal with what? What's going on?"

"Don't worry about it," he said. "We'll talk later."

I'm the type of person who wants to have that type of conversation now rather than later.

"You know what I'm already feeling," I told him, "so you might as well tell me."

"Well," he reluctantly said, "we have friends who are watching the news, and all over the news they're saying not to go to this Jeremy Camp event, that it's provocative in nature and that it's going to agitate people."

Oh, great. What are we doing here?

"The Ministry of Religion called us," Jed continued, "and they might cancel the whole event or allow you to play but limit you to only singing and not speaking between songs."

If that wasn't threatening enough, Jed told me that I needed to be careful what I said for the sake of the local pastor, Pasha, because the Ministry was holding him responsible for the event.

"They said if you say the wrong thing," Jed warned, "they'll put Pasha in prison for a year."

Fear started rising up within me. I was afraid of saying the wrong thing—and I wasn't clear on what "the wrong thing" would be—and knowing I could be responsible for Pasha being imprisoned was overwhelming.

I continued into the youth event burdened by uncertainty. As we led worship, I sensed a heavy, dark oppressiveness over the crowd. Plus, fear—within myself and within the youth.

After the band and I concluded playing, a former Miss Ukraine gave her testimony. An invitation for the youth to come forward for prayer was given, and dozens of young people came forward. As we were praying, I couldn't help but wonder what would happen to those youth after they left the concert and returned to their homes and lives.

I started singing a worship song, and immediately all the fear left the building. The wall of resistance came crashing down. I experienced an overwhelming sense of *We've got this. Through God's strength and His power, we can do this, no matter what's going to happen.* A load seemed to lift from the entire building. More youth started toward the front, where they all worshipped God in what turned out to be a beautiful moment.

After the event, we went out for dinner. I looked at Jed across the table and asked, "Should I watch my back?"

Jed is not dramatic in the least. But he answered, "Yeah, just be careful."

Then it struck me how my face was all over Bishkek; there would be no hiding.

Later that night, I called home to Adrienne. When she answered, all I said was, "Honey."

"Hi, my love," she said. "How are you?"

I started bawling.

"What's the matter?" she asked.

I described the evening to her.

"I don't know if this event's going to happen," I told her. "And if it does take place and I say the wrong thing, they're threatening to put Pasha in prison for a year."

"What?!"

"Yeah. I don't know what's going to happen. I want to come home. I'm ready to come home."

"Honey," she boldly said. "You were called for such a time as this. You're going to come home. But you're called to be there right now. I believe it with all my heart."

Adrienne's words rocked my world. When we ended the call, I said, "God, I can't do this. I'm too weak."

I could sense His words in reply: "Perfect. Now you're ready to do this."

I completely surrendered the rest of the trip to God, admitting I could not finish in my own strength. *That's right, you can't,* I sensed Him telling me. *I want you to speak only My words.*

Of course, that's what we want to do—always. But in those circumstances, that thought carried extra significance as the Lord was basically telling me, "Don't open your mouth unless I'm telling you to."

We had a day of rest before the final event, and, despite the success of the youth event, we had tempered our expectations for that concert. The government had issued its public warnings about our concert through the news. We'd received death threats, including a potential sniper attack and bombings. And the weather forecast called for rain the entire day of the concert.

We rallied our prayer team on the other side of the world. Meanwhile, that night our team and the local church leaders gathered for what became a time of powerful prayer. The local leaders had been praying for this moment for years—long before it was determined to ask us to come to their country. Jed has since described how that night he felt the concert would be the culmination of the work God had been doing in the hearts of the Kyrgyz people.

Life-Changing Experience

When we arrived at the stadium for our concert, picketers greeted us. The police had already hauled off one man, we were told, for making violent threats against us.

Emotions were high as the band members and I gathered to pray before the event, and let me assure you, our prayer covered everything from weather to snipers. The local bodyguard, whom, let's just say, I had become very close to in the past couple of days, entered the band's room. Fear blanketed his face.

"You okay?" I asked.

He placed his right hand on his chest and made the motion of a heart beating rapidly.

"A lot going down out there," he answered.

"Okay," I said.

"You go down, we go down together," he said in broken English.

I didn't know if he was trying to encourage me with that statement, but if that was his aim, he failed! I mean, I was glad he was willing to give his life to protect me, but mere minutes before going onstage, I was vigorously hoping that wouldn't be necessary!

As we left our room, I prayed, "Okay, God. This is all You."

On our walk to the stage, our group started singing a song of worship. I felt peace and joy. Then it was like I received an infusion of strength. Not my strength, but strength from God. I've seen a picture from when we were walking onto the stage. I looked like I didn't have a care in the world, and my bodyguard was in the foreground, surveying the crowd with an intense face. We could not have looked any more different. God's strength and power are amazing!

First, outside of a refreshing sprinkle right before the concert, it didn't rain. From the stage, I looked up into the sky to see dark, menacing clouds all around—except for above the stadium. It was like there was a weather blockade protecting the stadium.

Second, I felt as though I was 100 percent in tune with the Holy Spirit during the concert. I tend to talk a lot between songs during our concerts. That night, I shared only what I felt the Holy Spirit directly leading me to say.

About eight thousand came to the concert. The concert got off to a good start, but as soon as I sang the words, "Jesus, You are the way," a spontaneous exodus of about two thousand people occurred. It appeared as though a quarter of the audience had wanted to leave but was waiting on the first few to walk out. I watched them leave as we played. But I didn't change anything about what I was doing. When I felt the Holy Spirit prompting me to speak, I did. If I didn't feel His leading, I didn't talk. From a presentation standpoint, talking less than normal felt awkward to me, but I was determined not to say anything unless I had no doubt I was supposed to.

When we finished playing, Pasha took the microphone. He didn't mention the word *salvation*, but he said, "If you want to hear more about this Jesus, we have people here who will talk to you if you want."

I wanted to see the crowd's response, but security whisked us off the stage and immediately into a waiting car because of the threats against us. That seems weird even writing about it now, and I don't like the idea of dashing off as soon as we're finished at a concert. But in that situation, the best thing we could do was to remove the source of the threats—namely, me—and allow the local believers to minister to their people in the way they knew best to do.

In the car, my dad told me, "That is the most anointed I've ever heard you."

I can still to this day say that everything I said that night came from the Lord and that I didn't open my mouth unless He told me to. It was the most radical moment I've ever experienced. I believe that's because no matter how crazy the situation was or how dark the environment felt, I knew that God wanted me there and wanted me to share how my story glorifies Him. Like Adrienne had said on the phone, I was there in God's timing. I had plenty of doubts and concerns, from the time we decided to go to when I took the stage that night. But I also understood that when I run toward what God calls me to do, instead of running away, He's big enough to protect me regardless of what is going on around me.

God worked that night in Kyrgyzstan. I learned later that as we were leaving for the car, Pasha also told the crowd from that stage that "if this American can come and be so bold to share on this stage, then *we* need to stand up too."

From what I've heard, the outreach made a lasting impact on Bishkek. The way it has been told to me is that the people of Bishkek responded to the fact that an American musician left the safety of his country to come to their home and proclaim the gospel message. My version is that this American musician was terrified and not sure what he was doing there, but the Holy Spirit gave him the ability to do what God had called him to Kyrgyzstan to do. Any boldness I displayed came from God.

Jed and his family eventually had to leave Kyrgyzstan because their visas were not renewed in the aftermath of the concert. Now they are doing great work in the country of Georgia, and Paul and Melanie are serving in the Middle East.

I've had my share of life-changing experiences—there's nothing boring about my life! That trip to Central Asia became another. I have ministered in many countries, but Kyrgyzstan was the first place that was dangerous, that brought as much resistance as we faced. For the first time, I legitimately put my life at risk for the gospel.

It's one thing to be willing to risk your life, but it's entirely different to actually do so. Because I placed myself in a situation I had never experienced, I felt the presence of the Holy Spirit in a way I had never experienced. I returned home changed.

Chapter 20

THE FATHER'S
PERFECT LOVE

Following the trip to Kyrgyzstan, I was prepared to walk away from music.

I was without a record contract. We were fielding calls from record companies that wanted to sign me, and as we had conversations with the different companies, my focus was on not wanting to build Jeremy Camp's kingdom. I understand branding and marketing, and I appreciate the need to not only do them but do them well. Yet I was in a place where I was fully aware of how much around me was "Jeremy Camp this" and "Jeremy Camp that."

I was considering going independent instead of signing with a label. I also was considering making a dramatic shift in how I ministered. Our kids ranged in age from ten to three, and Egan, our youngest, was old enough that we could consider the possibility of pursuing ministry that involved more of the family.

The Kyrgyzstan experience and the risk I encountered there moved me into a position where I was willing to go wherever God wanted me to go. If God had told me that He wanted me to become a missionary, I would have quit music and prepared to sell our house and move to whatever country God called us to. Adrienne was absolutely on board as well.

I don't want to say I didn't care about music because that was not the case. But after Kyrgyzstan, I no longer cared what I would do for a living as long as it was what God wanted me to do. I still loved music, but I had a new willingness in my heart to follow God wherever He wanted me to go and for whatever He wanted me to do. If that meant no longer being a part of the music industry, that would have been totally cool. And I wasn't in a rush to figure out what was next. I was in a complete mind-set of, *God, whatever it is, all I know is that it has to be You.*

As Adrienne and I prayed for direction, I felt inspired to write songs even though I did not have a contract or an album to write for. My new songs came out of the Kyrgyzstan trip. "Same Power" was birthed out of reflecting on Kyrgyzstan and asking God, "How did I do all that while walking in fear amid that resistance?" Romans 8:11 came to mind: "And if the Spirit of him who raised Jesus from the dead is living in you, he who raised Christ from the dead will also give life to your mortal bodies because of his Spirit who lives in you."

That's it! That's it! I realized. That's what gave me the ability— His same strength, His same power, His same Spirit that allowed Christ to walk on water, to command the dead to wake and to rise from the grave. That same power lives within us!

I look back now and see that period of time coming out of the Kyrgyzstan trip sparked a spiritual growth spurt for me. More than taking a step forward, I believe I took a step of growth in depth because I laid everything down before the Lord's feet and said, "I'm willing to give it up. I'm ready to go wherever You want me." That was a radical, amazing season I look back on fondly.

Old Issues Reappear

After more prayer, I signed with Capitol Records. My first album under that contract was titled, appropriately enough, *I Will Follow*. We had sweet times singing "Same Power," along with the two other main songs from that album, "He Knows" and "Christ in Me." I felt fresh and empowered by the Holy Spirit. Assured that God wanted me to continue in music, I was full-on with that direction. In 2017, I wrote my next album, *The Answer*, and things were continuing to go well.

Then we heard from Kevin Downes again. He had stayed in touch with my manager, Matt, once a year or so, letting us know that he believed in my story and still wanted to make it into a movie. Each time I was like, *Cool. That'd be great—someday.* This time Kevin told me he was producing a movie with brothers Jon and Andy Erwin: *I Can Only Imagine*, the life story of my friend Bart Millard of MercyMe.

I still thought turning my story into a movie would be awesome because I knew God could use my testimony to touch many people. But I also knew that God would have to tell me when it was time.

Kevin contacted us more frequently than he had been, and a sense began growing in my spirit that the time was coming. Other than when Kevin and I first began talking to potential directors and writers, I hadn't thought that a movie would happen. Now that changed. With the movie likelihood growing, I reflected more on all I had been through in life and, really, started a journey back through those emotions and the pain.

At the same time, Adrienne and I had someone close to us battling addiction. With addiction, manipulation and deceit often appear, and that was definitely present in this case. Adrienne and

I both were deeply hurt because we had trusted and respected our friend. We struggled to process why this had happened and how it had become so bad. We struggled with knowing how to rebuild trust in a relationship severely damaged. I dropped back into a period of questioning, *God, what's happening here?* In addition to the distrust and pain from this situation, I was reliving the memories of Melissa's illness and her going to be with Jesus as I spent more time considering a movie.

The death of a spouse is traumatic, and the effects are long-lasting. They surface in unexpected ways. Reexperiencing that part of my life yet again while battling the circumstances surrounding Adrienne's and my friend, I slipped back into my issues with fear and trust. When those issues arise, I tend to take control of my situations even though I know my attempt to grab control actually is grabbing control away from God.

In January 2018, I took our daughters, Bella and Arie, to Uganda for a Speaking Louder Ministries outreach. It was a mixed trip for me since it was also the first time I was traveling alone with our kids without Adrienne. The girls had been praying for this opportunity for a whole year, and the outreach was incredible; God worked in amazing ways. Thirty-five thousand people showed up for our event in Kampala, the Ugandan capital. Our daughters were part of a move of God that saw a thousand people accept Christ as their Savior. I've been traveling to foreign countries for almost twenty years, and I'm still astounded when that many people give their hearts to the Lord. For my daughters to see that at their ages, man, it blows my mind to think with all the years they have ahead of them how such a moment might shape whatever their forms of ministry become as adults.

Our ministry's outreaches aren't just a concert. We travel to other countries to take the message that God brings hope, and we want that message to resound long after we've packed up and returned home. In Uganda we hosted a leadership conference for ministerial leaders from around Kampala. The discipleship training from that conference continues to echo throughout Uganda in the voices of the local ministers whose passion is to preach Christ to their own people. In the small city of Entebbe, we also built a medical clinic to meet the physical needs of the people, which, in turn, will open up hurting people's hearts so Jesus can bring the healing they most need—spiritual healing.

I am proud of the work of the people associated with our ministry. I'm thrilled that Bella and Arie could witness God change lives in Uganda. That was a beautiful trip. But it wasn't an easy trip for me. Physically, the best way I can describe it is that I felt weird. I was nervous the entire trip. I was paranoid that something would happen to my girls. I was fearful and untrusting; I wanted to control every situation while we were in Uganda.

I returned home exhausted.

Adrienne and I had scheduled a family trip to Italy, with plans to later lead worship for a tour in Rome and then Israel. Our family got sick in Italy on our vacation-only days. And as we went on to Israel, I didn't feel well. My chest felt tight at times, and one night I sensed a mild panic attack coming on. I managed to breathe through it and later forgot about it.

A couple of weeks after we returned home, Adrienne left the house for a few hours, and I started working out. All of a sudden the panic came back, but this time in full force—like nothing I had ever experienced. I called Adrienne, freaking out. Breathing became difficult. I didn't know what to do, so I lay on the floor until she came home and helped me calm down.

Following that day, I fell into a dark, crazy depression that lasted almost a solid week. Weird thoughts kept rushing at me, like *What if I die, and there's nothing?* Over those four days I felt as though I was losing my mind. I would get on the floor and call out to God.

Adrienne was constantly praying and battling alongside me. All I knew to do was to worship. I have led thousands and thousands of people in worship for years, and even worshipping was difficult for me. I would receive a little bit of a lift, but I felt like I was trying to climb my way out of a hole, and just as I began to make progress, the dirt in the side of the hole would give way and I would slide back down to the bottom.

Finally, one day as I prayed, God started revealing problem areas in my heart. He showed me how I was trying to control situations instead of following Him. He showed me how I was trusting in my own abilities—as limited as they were—instead of His. Reliving Melissa's illness and suffering was difficult. The betrayal of someone I loved and respected hurt deeply. God knew that. I started repenting for all the times I had tried to control situations—with my family, my wife, my career. I repented of any fear or unforgiveness in my heart. And God knew the exact words I needed to hear from Him in my depressed state: *I love you. Trust Me. Perfect love casts out fear. And My love is perfect for you.*

God reminded me of a moment a few years earlier when I had broken down and He had lifted me out of my hole and into His loving embrace.

Look at how faithful I've been to you. Look at what I've done for you. I love you.

Perfect love. That is not something we humans are capable of giving one another. But that's what God gives to us.

In that moment God wasn't mad at me. He wasn't demanding to know what was wrong with me or why I was bitter, trying be in control, and not trusting Him even though He had proved Himself to be so faithful to me so many times. No, instead, He told me that He loved me and that I could trust Him because He had the best plan for me. He wasn't telling me that I would not have to go through another hardship. That would be counter to what His Word tells us. But God was telling me that regardless of what I go through, He would always be there with me. And that He would always love me. Perfectly, as only He can.

Preventive Measures

The songs I wrote out of this experience make up most of what I consider my most vulnerable album since the first one following Melissa going to heaven. On the album titled *The Story's Not Over*, songs like the title track and "Father" came from me looking back on my life and struggles and remembering how God had worked in my life.

"Father" was me painting a beautiful picture of God being our heavenly Father and about trusting Him completely for our healing.

I can't say that God pulled me immediately out of that hole I was stuck in. The depression left, but remnants of the anxiety remained for several months as I relearned how to walk in daily trust of God as I opened my Bible, not just to read and get a nugget for that day but to bask in God's Word.

That was a necessary process for me to grow through. Although we would prefer an immediate rescue from our problems, I think God sometimes chooses to take us through a longer process because He has lessons for us to learn as we climb out of our holes. As He holds our hands and pulls us as we dig our toes into the side of the hole with each step, we experience more of His strength and learn more of His patience in bringing us out of situations in ways that are most beneficial to our relationship with Him.

In that case I realized that sometimes the best thing I can say to God is "I'm sorry."

I'm sorry, sincerely stated, is such a humbling phrase. Coming out of a phase in which I had chosen to trust myself over God, I needed to humble myself before Him.

I now believe that God was revealing those weaknesses to me for a reason. I had been on the mountaintop after Kyrgyzstan because I had seen His faithfulness in full display. But even when I could not imagine things going better, I remained susceptible to reverting back to my issues with fear and trust. Those are weaknesses, He reminded me, that the enemy will attack. I needed to make sure I protected myself in those areas for the next season He had planned for me.

Chapter 21

LIGHTS! CAMERA!
ACTION!

When *I Can Only Imagine* released in theaters in March 2018, Kevin, Matt, and I still were in the just-talking stage with my story. My impression was that Kevin understandably wanted to wait to see how Bart's movie would fare. *Imagine* shattered all expectations, grossing more than $15 million at the box office in its opening weekend alone. The success was well deserved; the movie was high quality.

Two weeks after *Imagine* released, Kevin called Matt and said he wanted to get together and start talking.

"We have to do this story," he said.

About that same time, the Erwin brothers and Kevin were launching their own faith-based movie studio called Kingdom Studios. We didn't make much progress because, behind the scenes, Kingdom Studios was trying to put together a deal with Lionsgate, which had distributed *Imagine* as well as other successful faith-based films like *Hacksaw Ridge* and *The Shack*.

During the waiting game, I wondered whether the movie would happen or not. I have discovered that getting an idea to the filming stage is the world's longest roller-coaster ride.

In time, Kevin told us that Kingdom was not sure if it wanted another music biopic for its next movie. They still wanted to make the film, he assured us, but another film likely would slide in between *Imagine* and mine.

Hey, I was super thankful just to have my story considered. I wondered, though, whether Kingdom striking a deal with Lionsgate would hurt my chances of having a movie. We had talked with Kevin for a few years and I knew where he stood with my story, but I knew nothing about Lionsgate, including whether they would even show an interest in making my story into a movie. That put us in another place of suspension, but I figured that if the movie was supposed to happen, it would.

The next time I heard from Kevin, he said the Erwin brothers wanted to meet with Adrienne and me and film us talking about the story. I had to schedule around road dates, and we were finally able to get together toward the end of summer.

I talked through the details of my story for a while, and then they asked Adrienne some questions. Adrienne told them, "When Melissa said if one person gives her life to Christ because of my death, it'll be worth it—it impacted me deeply. I am one of those people. I was not doing well, and God used her testimony to grip my heart."

When Adrienne concluded, Jon and Andy paused, looked at us, and said, "This story *has* to be told." They wanted to do my movie next. Later, they told me that answer from Adrienne convinced them to move my movie up on their list.

Next, Kevin and the Erwin brothers needed to take the idea to Lionsgate. We made an eight-minute sizzle reel—basically, a demo reel—to share the story for Lionsgate. I didn't know what to expect there. But it just so happened that one of Lionsgate's vice presidents was Bree Bailey, who grew up about thirty minutes from Lafayette, Indiana. She attended Purdue, and she knew about Pizza King and other places I liked to hang out while I was at Purdue. Bree was already familiar with my story and my music, and she pitched her full support.

Not only did Lionsgate decide to move forward with my movie, but they wanted it next.

Filming was scheduled to begin in May 2019 and be completed by the end of June. At that point, for the first time, after all the years of *hmm* and *no* and *maybe* and *maybe but when*, I realized the movie was actually going to happen. And that it was going to happen quickly!

The two biggest priorities were writing the script and assembling the cast.

The script writing began in January. Filming would begin in four months, and I was thinking, *Okay, is the script going to be finished in time?*

I had been told that although the story would be authentic, there would be a need to piece the story together. As with any movie I watch that is based on a true story, I expected *based on* to be the key words. Part of me anticipated the story being totally changed. So I was nervous when I received the first draft of the script. Adrienne and I started reading immediately, and we cried most of the way through. We used the same word to describe the script: *beautiful*. I was blown away by how accurately the script handled my story. Jon Erwin and Jon Gunn wrote it with the help of Madeline Carroll later in the process. They wrote verbatim words I had used when I recounted my story for them. I was impressed at how seriously the writers took remaining true to the story.

While we were going back and forth to finish the script, we began working on the cast.

Of course, you want actors and actresses with recognizable names to give the movie legitimacy. Around March, I was told that KJ Apa was under consideration to play me—a college-age me. I didn't know who KJ was, and they told me that he was a sought-after actor best known for starring in the TV series *Riverdale*. I wasn't familiar with that series either.

I was like, "Okay, cool."

They told me, "No, trust us, he is the guy. He is incredible. But it might be hard to get him."

So they were trying to land KJ, and I was praying, "God, if this is of You, You've just got to let it all happen."

By the grace of God, KJ signed on after reading the script and saying he wanted to be a part of the story. The moment we met him, we made an instant connection and became great friends.

Soon after we got KJ, Gary Sinise signed on to play my dad. Gary's was a name I knew. Getting Gary was incredible because he had won an Emmy and a Golden Globe and had been nominated for an Oscar.

For the role of Melissa, we knew we had to find someone KJ could connect with so they would have the right chemistry on-screen. About a hundred actresses tried out for the Melissa role, and there were some great and well-known actresses in that group. But the movie execs who were part of the interview process said none of them felt like the one who should portray Melissa.

After that round of auditions didn't produce a Melissa, KJ asked, "What about Britt Robertson?" I knew of Britt from the films *Dan in Real Life* and *Tomorrowland*. I thought, *Yeah, she'd be great!*

KJ and Britt had worked together for *A Dog's Purpose*, so KJ sent her a text. Then . . . crickets. When he did not receive a reply, he said, short and to the point, "Well, that's embarrassing."

Then KJ sent Britt a direct message via Instagram and said he was in a movie that he wanted to work with her in, and he asked her to check it out. He also mentioned he had tried to text her.

"I'm so sorry," Britt responded. "I got a different number."

KJ was relieved to hear that!

Britt read the script and said, "I have to do this."

When she signed, I was thinking, *Holy cow! This cast is amazing!* Then we added Melissa Roxburgh (*Manifest*) to play Melissa's older sister, Heather. Nathan Parsons, who plays the lead in the TV show *Roswell*, signed next as my friend and mentor Jean-Luc Lajoie. And then Shania Twain signed to play my mom, and Nicolas Bechtel and Reuben Dodd came aboard to play my brothers Jared and Josh, respectively.

Then we needed someone to play Adrienne. That turned out to be Abigail Cowen from *Stranger Things*. Adrienne and Abigail totally connected during the movie process, and it has been sweet to watch their friendship develop.

I was blown away by all the cast members' reactions after reading the script. This was a movie they all wanted to be a part of. The way assembling the cast went down to almost the last minute in some cases made me so glad I'm not in the movie industry. But without doubt, we had a cast that the Lord brought together. I remember thinking at some point while watching filming that I could not imagine the cast any different from the one we had working on our story.

The Next Chapter

I enjoyed being on set to watch the story come together through the amazing actors and actresses. I tried to stay out of the way and let the professionals do their jobs, but the cast and crew were gracious to Adrienne and me while we were there. Andy Erwin would ask me questions from time to time, and KJ asked me about specific ways I responded to or handled different parts of the story. They were completely committed to portraying every little detail correctly. That meant a great deal to both of us, to see our story handled with that level of respect and care.

I missed about half of filming because of my schedule, including completion of an album. I had to leave for a two-week stretch to attend a conference in Hawaii. Imagine being bummed about going to Hawaii!

The first day I returned to the set from Hawaii happened to be the day they filmed the hospital scene when Melissa thought she was healed and was trying to get out of bed. When Britt sat up in her hospital bed and exclaimed, "It's gone! It's gone!" I couldn't handle it. I turned and ran to find a place where I could break down and cry. Adrienne followed me off the set and held me until I could gather my emotions.

The hospital scene was too real for me, like watching it actually happen. I have talked about what took place in the hospital many times, but other than in my mind's memories, that was the first time since it happened that I *saw* Melissa try to get out of bed.

Melissa's death also was on the shooting schedule, and I did not return to the set that day. They record several takes of each scene when making a movie, and I could not subject myself to watching those scenes over and over.

Overall, witnessing my life unfold before me on a movie set was a surreal experience. Adrienne and I would watch and mention to each other that we could not have imagined this movie would actually take place. Being on set especially caused me to realize that Melissa's heart to reach one person had become this massive ministry that had already reached millions of people and, through the movie, would reach millions more.

I try to live in a manner that is openhanded to whatever God wants to do in my life, and to feel that God was entrusting me with this next season of a movie to share His story again was extremely humbling. Thankfulness was a big part of my emotions—thankfulness for what God had done to bring me to that point, and thankfulness that He had prepared me for all that would result from the movie.

The success of Bart Millard's movie created the path for *I Still Believe* to be filmed. Bart is a trusted friend, and he generously gave me some of his time so that we could sit down together and talk about not only the movie process but also what I could anticipate after the movie released. If you haven't seen the film *I Can Only Imagine*, I highly recommend you do. Part of Bart's story includes living with an abusive father. Bart openly described for me how the movie process triggered some of the father issues he still carried, and how watching the filming brought up emotions he discovered he still needed to figure out.

He told me, "Man, get ready for people to share their story after story with you. And be prepared to wear that heavy weight on your shoulders."

I've encountered that to a degree through my book and sharing my testimony in concerts. Bart told me I need to prepare for that experience on a greater scale because of the number of people the movie will reach.

He also told me that I would receive even more invitations to speak about my experiences with grief than I already do. He told me that I would not feel like I was expert enough to speak on grief and would have uncertainties about whether I should even place myself in those positions. But then he gave me great advice: "Just do the things that you feel like God wants you to do. Don't just do things because the door is open. Make sure it's something that He wants you to do."

I needed to hear those words in particular. God has shown me numerous times that not all good things are God things, that because a door is open and it seems like a good thing doesn't necessarily mean He wants me to do that.

From talking with Bart, I believe that, moving forward, a good litmus test for me will be whether I feel a peace about the opportunities that come my way. I appreciate Bart's wisdom and his willingness to share it with me.

I don't look forward to telling people no when opportunities to talk further about the movie and my story come. I know ahead of time that there will be more opportunities than I can accept. I also have to take care of myself, and I have to take care of my family.

Adrienne . . . wow! I owe her so much. At any point if she had said, "I don't think I can handle this movie," that would have been all I needed to hear. Since we met eighteen years ago, she has embraced my testimony. She has encouraged me to talk about Melissa. At times she was the one championing me to talk about Melissa because she so believes in the power of my testimony and God's faithfulness through it all.

She has always been supportive, and that did not change during the movie process. Watching her on the set encouraging everybody remains a highlight for me. The cast and crew were telling me, "Your wife is amazing." I'd say, "I know!"

Adrienne and I have been married for sixteen years. We have three growing children. Yet we realize there will be a point during the movie when viewers are going to fall in love with Jeremy and Melissa. They are going to be disappointed that Melissa and I couldn't live our lives together.

Adrienne has told me, "I know that I know that I know that God is going to use this movie, and that's all that really matters. It's not about me. But I'm not naive. I know the possibility of how people will react to your love story with Melissa. I've had moments when I've thought about that. It's not an easy feeling, but I'm asking the Lord to prepare my heart and to help me handle it all with His grace. And I know that we're supposed to do this, and I want people to hear what God has done in your life."

Amazing. And I would love for Adrienne to be honored through this movie.

But most of all, I want to honor God because His perfect love has taught me how to love and how to be loved.

Chapter 22

I STILL BELIEVE

Faith and family. My story always seems to come back to that.

My parents are still in Lafayette and still pastoring the same church they started about twenty-five years ago. Harvest Chapel has earned a reputation as a church that ministers to the down-and-out of its city. It's amazing to see what the Lord has done in and through that church, and how He has blessed my parents for their faithfulness to Him.

My sister, April, is married with four awesome kids and has her own powerful testimony of God's grace and mercy. When I left home for college, April was still doing her own thing but to much greater extremes than what I had done. Frankly, her life was a mess. While I was at Bible college, I would literally get on my face on the floor and pray, "God, please bring my sister back to You." It took a while—not until after I had finished college—but she fully recommitted her life to Christ, and her husband, Trent, gave his life to the Lord too. They have been faithfully serving the Lord alongside my parents. Trent is the worship leader, and my sister runs the church coffee shop that reaches out to their local community.

My brother Jared married the most amazing girl named Heather, and they have four incredible kids. Jared and I are eight years apart in age, and because I spent my junior high and part of my high school years chasing my own desires, I wasn't as close to my brother as I could have been when I left for college. I was living out in California and beginning to tour with my music. But eventually Jared and I were able to establish a close relationship. He's a gifted guitar player and has played in our band. He is currently the worship pastor at our church in California. Traveling together, when he was with the band, gave us an opportunity to make up for lost time. I hope I've been able to be the big brother to him I wasn't for too many years, and that I encourage him in the gifts God has given him.

Joshua—what a special young man. He was born with Down syndrome and was only eight years old when I moved off to college, so I didn't get to spend much time with him, either, as he grew up. Josh has always had so much joy. I remember he would be sick and my mom would say, "Joshua, let's pray that you feel better." My mom would pray, and right away Josh would say, "Oh, I feel better!"

I've learned so much from Josh about having a childlike faith because, in those instances when he was sick, trusting was simple for him—my mom would pray, and God would heal him. There was nothing more to it than that. I also loved watching him interact with people. He would go up to someone at church and hug them and love on them, and his face would shine with just the most beautiful smile. Although he has had many health struggles and we don't often get to see him very joyful anymore, there will be a day when my little brother will be freed from the limitations of Down syndrome. I can't wait to see him in the presence of our Lord, where he will be able to experience the fullness of understanding and an even deeper joy than he has had on his best days in the past.

When Adrienne and I moved from Lafayette to near Nashville in 2007, I think moving away from my family might have been more difficult initially for Adrienne than for me! She and my mom had developed a sweet Ruth-Naomi relationship. The Bible says that a man will leave his father and his mother and should cleave unto his wife, but she had become so close to my parents that she has joked that she felt like she was the one leaving and cleaving.[22] It was such a great season of growth for us, though, as we learned to establish our own family.

Adrienne met Melissa's sisters, Megan and Heather, in California before we married; they became friends and have stayed in contact with one another over the years. Adrienne sent Melissa's parents flowers and a letter for a few of the anniversaries of Melissa's passing. They sent us a wedding gift and then baby gifts for Bella and Arie. When Adrienne and our daughters met Melissa's parents, Mark and Janette, for the first time, they were very sweet to Adrienne.

God has been so good to me and has blessed me with a wonderful family. I pray that the world will be so unappealing for my kids that as they grow older and come face-to-face with some of the worldly pleasures I foolishly pursued, they'll say, "That's gross—I don't want that."

Adrienne released two solo albums but for now has not chosen to make an all-out launch of a solo career. From time to time, she thinks about recording songs that are meaningful to her and can be an encouragement to others, and she might dabble in music again, but she has since taken up writing. She has written two books. We both feel that after the movie we are supposed to do more things together. We don't know yet exactly what that means. But we have cowritten a marriage book titled *In Unison*, scheduled to be released at the same time as the movie. To me, one of the best things about our kids growing up is that Adrienne and I have had opportunities to minister together. I admire how Adrienne has put her career somewhat on hold so that she could place most of her focus on being a mom—and she's a great one. She homeschools our children so that she and the kids can have flexibility to travel with me at times. As much as I enjoy being out on tour, I dislike much more being away from my family. In general, if

I am going to be on the road for more than a week, my family will travel with me so we're not apart for too long. Sometimes they travel with me on shorter trips.

As adults, Adrienne and I can talk by phone and still maintain good communication. (After all, we did that most of the time we were engaged.) It's not the most effective way to communicate, but I believe God has given us a special grace and mercy in our marriage to carry out what we are meant to be doing for Him.

But my kids need their dad's presence, not just his voice over the phone. They need me to be with them and interact with them. They need to watch me be an example for them.

When the kids were much younger and I would go out on the road and Adrienne and the kids would stay home, Adrienne would pray with them at night and tell them, "Daddy is telling people about Jesus, and we'll get to see them all in heaven one day."

That turned into them asking me, "Did you tell people about Jesus, Dad?" Isn't that awesome? Now, they're older and don't ask me that anymore, but they are still fully supportive of our family making sacrifices in order to share what God has done in our lives.

When Bella was little, I was talking with her and said, "I love you so much."

"More than Jesus?" she asked.

"Nope," I told her.

Bella gave me the sweetest look and said, "That's okay. I know you're supposed to love Jesus more."

I am blessed to be able to share my career with my family.

Because Adrienne has done the whole tour routine herself—multiple times—she understands how crazy the schedule on the road can become. She totally gets the business side of the music industry. There have been times when the family is on the road with me and she'll see the schedule starting to get to me. "Hey," she'll tell me, "if it gets too crazy, we'll go home and let you do your thing," or she'll give me space and tell me not to worry about them. She is an extraordinarily selfless woman.

This isn't a biased comment, because I was saying this way back on the Festival Con Dios tour when there was not a hint of a spark between us, but Adrienne has also been gifted with a beautiful singing voice. (And the cutest South African accent when she talks too!)

She often is my backup singer onstage and on CDs, and there is something truly special about sharing my testimony of what I went through with Melissa, telling the stories behind "Walk by Faith" and "I Still Believe," and then singing those songs with Adrienne. Sometimes as we perform, I feel that God has graciously granted me a sense of completeness.

Not surprisingly, I get asked a lot of questions about Melissa and Adrienne. It's difficult to describe, but it's like my heart didn't have to push one out for the other. Instead, it was like my heart expanded so it could have room for both. And now that Adrienne and I have been married for sixteen years, there's no comparison at all. Not that there ever was, but Adrienne is the one whom God has given me to walk with in this life. It blows me away sometimes when I think about it.

But then a lot of things God has done in my life blow me away. He is an awesome God! How could I not want to tell everyone I can about Him?

I can recall my thoughts way back on the Christmas morning when I opened my Taylor guitar. They remain my mission today: *Lord, whatever You want. Not my plans, but Yours. Here I am.*

My Desire

I've been asked for my definition of worship. My answer is "anything we do that glorifies the Lord." One interviewer who asked me that question said my answer surprised him because he expected a musician would give a music-related answer.

I've heard worship defined as "worship songs that are sung to the Lord" or "songs we sing in church on Sunday mornings." But worship is so much broader than music. Worship can be something as simple as a conversation. If I'm with someone and we're talking about the Lord and what He has done in our lives, if we are lifting up His name, I consider that worshipping God.

The worship project was my first opportunity to work with a label. After that, I became grouped into the Christian rock segment of our industry. Then later my music began to be labeled again more as adult contemporary music. I've played different styles of songs, but as far as I'm concerned, I've always been a worship musician. Perhaps more accurately, I've always considered myself a *worshipping* musician.

One of my songs is called "My Desire." I'm frequently asked to explain the source of the depth of my music, but "My Desire" has a rather simple message. As one line says, "This is my desire, to be used by You."

That's it. That's my desire—to be used by God.

The reason is expressed best in two lines near the song's end:

> There's not much I can do to repay all You've done,
> So I give my hands to use.[23]

My hands are vital to my calling. I play the guitar with them. I write songs with them. So when I say I give my hands to God for Him to use as He wishes, I mean that literally. But more so than my hands, I give my heart to God.

I want to write songs that touch God's heart. I believe that when God sees one of His children writing songs of love for his Father— songs that glorify Him—His heart is touched. To me, songs written from the heart are real. They are honest. They are emotionally raw. When I am honest and say, "Okay, God, this is how I'm feeling," I open my heart to Him so that He can do a transforming work within me.

God called David a man after His own heart, not because David was perfect, but because he was repentant.[24] Read through David's psalms; it's obvious that he was honest with God about his thoughts and feelings, and look at the work God did within David.

That is where I want to be in my relationship with God—where my heart is opened completely so that He can mold and shape me as He wants. I want my music to help others find that openness in their relationship with God too.

That is my desire.

Another song we sing includes the words *We'll sing it out to let all the world know that Jesus saves.* Over the past few years, the Lord has allowed us to take that message into new areas, including international shows in more than forty countries.

I've learned that whether the audience is in a foreign country hearing my words through a translator or scrolling through their Instagram feeds, more people than we could even fathom need to hear how God has helped us through life's deepest valleys so they can be encouraged to stand firm and say, "We have to believe!"

But to be honest, there have been nights, especially in the early years after Melissa went to heaven, when I would be preparing to go onstage fully aware that many in the audience had come to hear me share my story and then sing "I Still Believe," yet I didn't want to sing it. I knew the words were true, but they didn't feel true.

I would tell God, *I don't feel like You're good. I don't feel like You're faithful.* On those nights, it was a true step of faith to say, *Okay, God, even though I don't feel it, I'm still going to sing it.* I could say that because of the times in my life when, at moments I didn't expect, God had come through for me. On those nights when I put aside what I didn't feel and sang what I knew to be true, I saw God move in mighty ways among the people in the audience.

In more recent years there were nights when I would think, *I can't sing this song tonight because I'm not trusting the Lord right now!* Or I would ask myself, *How can I tell these people that "I still believe" when I'm fearing what might happen next in my life?* But strengthened by the previous times when I had trusted God and sang "I Still Believe" anyway, I stepped out onto the stage and sang it from my heart. Every time I've done that, God has amazed me with how many hearts He touches through the song, and for me to have done otherwise would have been to allow the enemy to claim a victory.

The story of what I went through with Melissa is not just a story; it is my testimony. And "I Still Believe" is not just a song; it is my battle cry.

It has been almost twenty years since that day on my parents' couch when, even though I didn't want to, I picked up my guitar, and "I Still Believe" flooded into my heart.

(Verse 1)
Scattered words and empty thoughts
Seem to pour from my heart
I've never felt so torn before
Seems I don't know where to start
But it's now that I feel Your grace fall like rain
From every fingertip, washing away my pain

(Verse 2)
Though the questions still fog up my mind
With promises I still seem to bear
Even when answers slowly unwind
It's my heart I see You prepare
But it's now that I feel Your grace fall like rain
From every fingertip, washing away my pain

[Bridge]
The only place I can go is into Your arms
Where I throw to You my feeble prayers
In brokenness I can see that this was Your will for me
Help me to know You are near

[Chorus]
I still believe in Your faithfulness
I still believe in Your truth
I still believe in Your holy Word
Even when I don't see, I still believe[25]

I could not have expressed those words on my own. Lost in a deep valley, feeling alone and unable to even stand on my own, I looked up from my fog to see my loving God there with me, hand outstretched to help me back to my feet so He could begin walking me through to the other side of my despair.

My journey was not easy. In fact, my journey still continues and will continue until that promised day of "no more death or mourning or crying or pain." Along the way, God has placed wonderful people into my life who have helped me reach the point where I am now. But more than that, God has placed Himself into my life. He has walked alongside me every step of the way. I didn't always recognize Him near, but looking back from this side of my despair, I now do.

I know that many of you who hear or read the lyrics of "I Still Believe" can say, "That is where I am right now." My heartfelt prayer for each of you is that you will discover the hope and the healing from the Lord that has carried me. I have been seemingly stuck in that same valley at times. Like the Lord used Jon Courson to speak to me in his Oregon home, I can also tell you that God provides a way out of that valley.

I wish I could tell you when you will leave that valley. But I can't.

Everyone is different. We all deal with our circumstances differently. But we have a God who deals with us on an individual level. He created each of us, and He created you with a specific plan designed just for you. Embrace the people God brings into your life to help you through your difficulties. And embrace God. You might be wondering, as I did, if He hears you. If He really cares about your every situation. If He is even near to you. Trust me, He does hear your cries and groans and moans. He does care about you. He is near to you— He's right there alongside you.

So stand up and worship Him. Right now. Don't wait until you've crossed through to the other side. God is worthy of your praise at all times. Don't miss out on an opportunity to glorify Him in the midst of uncertainty. Your circumstances might be bad, but God is always good. Open your heart to God, tell Him in all honesty how you feel, and then discover the depths of how He can use you, even when you don't feel usable.

I've been there, and I can't imagine ever wanting to go back to that place. But now I am so thankful that through the pain, the loneliness, the confusion, the agony, God was there with me—growing me, maturing me, loving me, tenderly bringing me closer to Him. This life is full of disappointment and pain, but God is faithful.

That is why even when I cannot see, I can stand and sing, "I still believe."

I *do* still believe.

And because of what God has brought me through, I *will* believe.

NOTES

1. "I Still Believe," lyrics by Jeremy Camp, © 2002 Stolen Pride Music (ASCAP) Thirsty Moon River Publ. Inc. (ASCAP) (adm. at CapitolCMGPublishing.com). All rights reserved. Used by permission.

2. Hebrews 4:12.

3. Ezekiel 36:24–32.

4. Matthew 7:24–29.

5. Philippians 1:21.

6. Nehemiah 8:10.

7. 1 Thessalonians 5:18.

8. "Walk by Faith," lyrics by Jeremy Camp, © 2002 Stolen Pride Music (ASCAP) Thirsty Moon River Publ. Inc. (ASCAP) (adm. at CapitolCMGPublishing.com). All rights reserved. Used by permission.

9. "Revive Me," lyrics by Jeremy Camp, © 2004 Stolen Pride Music (ASCAP) Thirsty Moon River Publ. Inc. (ASCAP) (adm. at CapitolCMGPublishing.com). All rights reserved. Used by permission.

10. Matthew 21:12–13.

11. "Breaking My Fall," lyrics by Jeremy Camp, © 2002 Stolen Pride Music (ASCAP) Thirsty Moon River Publ. Inc. (ASCAP) (adm. at CapitolCMGPublishing.com). All rights reserved. Used by permission.

12. Proverbs 27:17.

13. Matthew 18:3.

14. 1 John 4:8.

15. 1 Peter 1:6.

16. Matthew 28:18–20.

17. John 10:10.

18. "Beyond Measure," lyrics by Jeremy Camp, © 2006 Stolen Pride Music (ASCAP) Thirsty Moon River Publ. Inc. (ASCAP) (adm. at CapitolCMGPublishing.com). All rights reserved. Used by permission.

19. 2 Corinthians 1:4 NKJV.

20. "There Will Be a Day," lyrics by Jeremy Camp, © 2008 Stolen Pride Music (ASCAP) Thirsty Moon River Publ. Inc. (ASCAP) (adm. at CapitolCMGPublishing.com). All rights reserved. Used by permission.

21. George Thomas, "Secret Believers Share Faith Under Fire," *CBN News*, January 23, 2015, https://www1.cbn.com/cbnnews/world/2013/june/secret-believers-share-faith-under-fire.

22. Genesis 2:24.

23. "My Desire," lyrics by Jeremy Camp, © 2004 Stolen Pride Music (ASCAP) Thirsty Moon River Publ. Inc. (ASCAP) (adm. at CapitolCMGPublishing.com). All rights reserved. Used by permission.

24. Acts 13:22.

25. "I Still Believe," lyrics by Jeremy Camp, © 2002 Stolen Pride Music (ASCAP) Thirsty Moon River Publ. Inc. (ASCAP) (adm. at CapitolCMGPublishing.com). All rights reserved. Used by permission.

ABOUT THE AUTHOR

JEREMY CAMP is a musician with forty number-one radio hits, four RIAA-certified Gold albums, and more than five million albums sold. He has been nominated for a Grammy, three American Music Awards, and four ASCAP Songwriter of the Year awards. He lives with his wife, Adrienne, and their three children in Tennessee.